Buzzed

Beers, Booze & Coffee Brews

rewery

Where to Enjoy the   d

New England Distilling,
spices for gin

To Corinne, who postponed our honeymoon
for this journey; my dad, who taught me to appreciate
great beer, coffee, and liquor; and to my mom,
who gave up her favorite drink in the world for
that nine-month period prior to my birth.

BUZZED
First Islandport edition/June 2016

*The author and the publisher encourage readers to visit the breweries, distilleries,
and coffee houses to sample their drinks, but we strongly recommend that those who
consume any alcoholic beverages travel with a designated nondrinking driver or make
arrangements to stay overnight in town rather than traveling.*

Thank you to all the businesses that supplied photos for this book.

ISBN: 978-1-939017-65-9
Library of Congress Control Number: 2014959882

Islandport Press
PO Box 10
Yarmouth, Maine 04096
www.islandportpress.com
books@islandportpress.com

Publisher: Dean L. Lunt
Book Design: Teresa Lagrange

Printed in the USA

Front cover images, top: Source Coffeehouse. Bottom: New England Distilling (left), Hill Farmstead
Brewery (photo by Bob M. Montgomery Images). Back cover image: Four Quarters Brewing.

Inside cover (left to right), top row: Rising Tide Brewing Company (photo by Foreside Photography),
Blue State Coffee. Middle row: Brass Lantern Inn (photo by Jumping Rocks), Allagash Brewing Company,
Harpoon Brewery. Bottom row: Hill Farmstead Brewery (photo by Bob M. Montgomery Images),
Two Roads Brewing Company, Cisco Brewers.

Inside back cover (left to right), top row: Flag Hill, Kents Falls Brewing Company. Middle row: Source
Coffeehouse, Bully Boy Distillers. Bottom row: Cask Republic (photo by Noah Fecks), Poverty Lane
Orchards & Farnum Hill Cider (photo by Brenda Bailey Collins).

Buzzed

Beers, Booze, & Coffee Brews

ISLANDPORT PRESS

Acknowledgements

This book would not have been written without Josh Pahigian, author of several classic books on baseball and travel, and the Maine thriller, *Strangers on the Beach*. Josh was a professor of mine while I was a student in Western Connecticut State University's MFA in creative and professional writing program.

Before one semester, we met to discuss our upcoming class. The meeting was at a Connecticut pizzeria with a surprisingly good beer list. Though I was well over twenty-one at the time, I wasn't sure if ordering a beer was appropriate during a school meeting. However, that beer list got the better of me, and I ordered a brewski. I can't recall what I ordered, but I do remember asking the waitress questions about a few on-tap offerings. Evidently, my love of beer was obvious and made an impression on Josh, who, after seeing some of my travel and food writing, recommended me to Islandport Press. Throughout this project, Josh has served as a mentor, guide, and resource on all things book-related, from business, to writing mechanics, to time management. Thanks again, Josh; I literally couldn't have done it without you.

I'd also like to thank Genevieve Morgan and the staff at Islandport Press for having enough faith in a first-time author to give me a cash advance and then send me off into the craft-beverage wilds of New England, trusting that at the end of eighteen months—and dozens of brewery, distillery, and coffee- house stops— I'd have an actual book to show for my efforts.

Also, special thanks to Lyn Hottes. I met Lyn when I was a nineteen-year-old intern at my first newspaper job. Ever since, she's been my most trusted second set of eyes, and an unceasing source of grammar and writing wisdom who has constantly donated her time, energy, and considerable talents in a successful (I hope) effort to make me a better writer.

Finally, thanks to my coworkers at *Connecticut Magazine* who let me take more than my fair share of long weekends over the past year; my family members and MacTalla Mor bandmates, Harry, Patty, Ilana, Jesse, and Levon, who agreed to cut back on touring as I researched this book (they were perhaps bribed by the promise of future brewery and distillery gigs); Adam Kaner and Amanda Moody, who allowed me to crash in their spare bedroom during the Boston-area legs of my travels; and all the brewers, baristas, roasters, distillers, bartenders, and craft-beverage team members I met along the way. It is a great honor and constant joy to drink products prepared with such sincerity, care, and skill.

Beer he drank–seven goblets.
His spirit was loosened . . . His heart was glad and his face shone.

—From the *Epic of Gilgamesh*, 3000 BC

Ho! Ho! Ho! To the bottle I go
To heal my heart and drown my woe.

—J. R. R. Tolkien

No one can understand the truth until he drinks
of coffee's frothy goodness.

—Sheikh Abd-al-Kadir

Table of Contents

Connecticut and Rhode Island

Vermont

Glossary

Four Quarters Brewing

Introduction

There would be blood.

On a fateful day in 1855, Celtic residents of Portland, Maine, took to the streets of the colonial fishing city with fury in their hearts. They didn't actually shout, *Braveheart*-style, "You may take our lives, but you may never take our alcohol!," but that was their message. They wanted their beer and alcohol back—products that Mayor Neal Dow had taken from them.

Dow, nicknamed the Napoleon of Temperance, was a leading Prohibitionist. In 1851, he had pushed through the so-called Maine Law, outlawing the sale of alcohol. Many of Portland's Celtic residents saw the law as discriminatory against them, their history, and their culture.

So on June 2, 1855, after the citizens of Portland learned that Dow was holding large quantities of alcohol purportedly for medical purposes (alcohol still could be used medicinally), an Irish-led mob gathered outside the building where the alcohol was being stored. Dow lived up to his Napoleon nickname when he responded to the mob like a ruthless general, ordering the militia to fire into the crowd. When the dust had settled, one man, John Robins, was dead, and seven others were wounded.

This unfortunate incident, known as the Portland Rum Riot, demonstrates a simple fact: We New Englanders are passionate about our beverages. More than 150 years later, that passion still can be felt in New England breweries, distilleries, and coffeehouses that are riding the crest of the alcohol- and caffeine-fueled craft-beverage wave. This book is an ode to some of the best craft-beverage destinations in New England, and a guide for those who want to experience them firsthand.

It all began a year and a half ago with an unexpected offer.

It sounded too good to be true—like one of those e-mails you get from a prince in a country you've never heard of promising fortunes beyond your wildest dreams if you send them a few hundred dollars. Based on the recommendation of my friend and former professor, author Josh Pahigian, the publishing company Islandport Press contacted me to ask if I would be interested in writing a book on craft beer.

"Yes," I said. "I think I might be."

Craft beer, coffee, and spirits may not *actually* be in my DNA, but they were certainly a big part of my upbringing. My father is a naturopathic doctor and my mother is a nurse practitioner. My parents were ravenous "locavores" before the term was coined and later painfully overused. As a natural extension of a diet of whole wheat, organic, and locally grown products, my parents, particularly my dad, were (and still are) on a seemingly constant quest for craft-beverage perfection.

Growing up, our basement was filled with glass jugs of fermenting home-brewed beer that my dad and family friend Bill Gillespie made; making coffee was an intense ritual that sometimes took half a day; and my parents' liquor cabinet was filled with hard-to-find spirits that were so rare they should probably have been kept in a safe. I still get nervous going near it.

There also were trips and craft-beverage excursions. As a kid I played at McNeill's Brewery in Brattleboro, overheard political debates at Caffe Kilim in New Hampshire, and was part of so many liquid-themed detours and trips that I couldn't count them now if I tried.

As you've probably guessed, somewhere along the way I caught the craft-beverage bug myself. Touring North America as a member the Celtic roots band MacTalla Mor and eating and drinking professionally as a staff writer at *Connecticut Magazine*, I've been lucky enough to indulge in more than my fair share of craft beverages. I've brought flights of beer onstage with me at craft-beer festivals in Canada, sipped sunshine-flavored beer at Florida

New England Distilling

breweries, drunk scotch with executives from some of Scotland's biggest whiskey companies in a Las Vegas nightclub, and kicked back, relaxed, and recharged while searching for the perfect cappuccino (my favorite coffee beverage) and pour-over coffee at shops up and down the East Coast.

So, when Islandport Press contacted me, I felt like I'd already been researching the topic for quite some time. Initially, the book was supposed to be solely about breweries. But as I began to explore the region's breweries in depth, I found myself also intrigued by local coffeehouses and distilleries and started making unscheduled stops at these *other* craft-beverage destinations.

That's when I noticed something peculiar. As I traveled from a brewery to a coffeehouse, or from a distillery to a brewery, I'd see many of the same faces at each location. There clearly were other liquid vacationers traveling from one craft-beverage hot spot to another. Evidently I was not the only one equally drawn to the three distinct, yet somehow linked, forms of beverages.

I began to question the wisdom of limiting the scope of the book to breweries: Why not expand it to include the brewing world's natural relatives? I ran the new idea by the team at Islandport, and they enthusiastically agreed to an expanded book that would cover more than breweries.

This book couldn't have been written without the help of my craft-beverage copilot and wife, Corinne Ofgang, who, immediately following our wedding, agreed to postpone a traditional honeymoon and instead joined me in my year-and-a-half-long search for craft-beverage nirvana in the big cities and quiet back roads of New England. (It was only later that I informed her she'd be serving as the designated driver on these trips.)

From my eighteen months researching this book, I remember beers so good I still dream about them, coffees with such enchanting subtleties of flavor I ran out of words to describe them, and spirits that filled *my* spirit with joy. I also remember the beauty of the journey—the way the sun set over a farm in northern Vermont; the music of street performers drifting over historic streets after midnight in Portsmouth, New Hampshire; the lights of fishing boats shining off in the distance like something out of a Hemingway novel, glimpsed briefly on the late-night ferry ride back to the mainland from Nantucket; and the crisp refreshing sea air blowing off the ocean waters outside of Portland, Maine.

And I remember the people I met along the way: men and women standing behind counters and taproom bars or in the shadow of silver fermenters—

passionate brewers, baristas, distillers, and entrepreneurs—the real-life characters making the drinks I love. In the pages that follow I've tried to bottle some of their spirit as well as the spirit of the local flavor I was lucky enough to sample along the way.

I hope you have half as much fun reading this book as I did researching and writing it, and that it inspires you to embark on some craft-beverage adventures of your own. And if somewhere in your travels, at the end of a quiet bar in an out-of-the-way brewery, you happen to see a thirty-something writer with black hair and a short beard, scribbling furiously into a notebook while a blonde woman who seems way out of his league tells him he's sampled enough different drinks for the day, come up and say hello. I'd love to buy you a drink.

Cheers, and bon voyage!

—Erik Ofgang

Suggested Itineraries

Below are some sample itineraries that will help get you started on your explorations. Just be warned: These sample trips have been designed with maximum craft-beverage immersion in mind, and while blazing through breweries and distilleries can be fun (I obviously love it), there's also nothing wrong with taking more time at a given destination and really slowing down and smelling the hops.

ONE-WEEK ITINERARY
New Hampshire, Maine, and Vermont

A week may sound like a long time, but it's barely enough to get a substantial taste of the craft-beverage scene in New Hampshire, Maine, and Vermont, which together form the unofficial holy trinity of New England craft culture. This weeklong trip will take you into the heart of the local beverage world and leave you craving more.

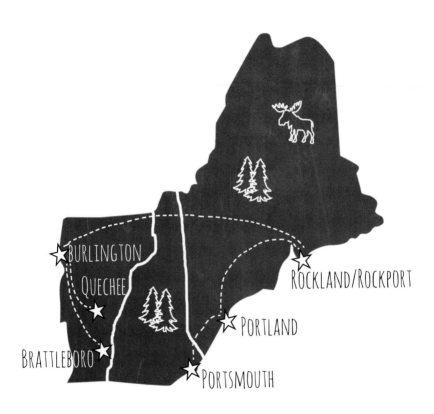

BURLINGTON

QUECHEE

ROCKLAND/ROCKPORT

PORTLAND

BRATTLEBORO

PORTSMOUTH

DAY 1   Portsmouth, New Hampshire

Start your craft-beverage adventure off right with a stop at the quirky, cool, and delicious **Caffe Kilim**, a place where modern US hippie culture meets ancient Middle Eastern coffee tradition. After you've caffeinated, explore Portsmouth's beautiful downtown on foot before heading just outside of town to **Sea Hagg Distillery** in North Hampton. After a few samples and a tour, head back downtown where you can top off your evening at **Earth Eagle Brewings**, one of the most innovative small breweries in New England.

DAY 2   Embrace the Smutt

Start Day 2 with a downtown trip to **Portsmouth Book & Bar**, where you can browse books while enjoying excellent coffee and choosing from a cool selection of craft brews (don't drink too much, because there's a lot to do today!). Head about eighteen miles outside of Portsmouth to **Flag Hill**, a winery and distillery in Lee. Here you can tour the beautiful vineyard grounds and enjoy samples from one of New Hampshire's oldest modern distilleries. You'll also want to try the wine. Next head to **Smuttynose Brewing Company** in Hampton and plan on spending a few hours at this large brewing complex designed to be a day-trip attraction. After the free tour you can walk over to the brewery-owned **Hayseed Restaurant** which now features a nine-hole disc golf course to work off your meal.

The Places

New Hampshire
Caffe Kilim
Sea Hagg Distillery
Earth Eagle Brewings
Portsmouth Book & Bar
Flag Hill Distillery
Smuttynose Brewing Co.
Hayseed Restaurant

Maine
Rising Tide Brewing Co.
Maine Craft Distilling
Coffee By Design
Bunker Brewing Co.
Tandem Coffee Roasters
Speckled Ax
New England Distlling
Allagash Brewing Co.
Maine Beer Co.
Oxbow Brewing Co.
Sweetgrass Farm Winery
& Distillery
Rock City Café

Suggested Itineraries

Smuttynose Brewing Co.

DAY 3   **Portlandia**

Prepare yourself because things are about to get intense. Depart from Portsmouth and drive an hour north to one of the centers of New England craft beverages, Portland, Maine. This city is brimming with coffee, beer, and spirits. First stop is a neighborhood that some locals refer to as the "beverage district" or "yeast side." In a shared parking lot you'll find **Rising Tide Brewing Company** and **Maine Craft Distilling** across the street from **Coffee By Design** and the company's roasting facility. If time allows, head to the nearby **Bunker Brewing Company** and **Tandem Coffee Roasters**, which also share a parking lot.

DAY 4   **All-agash In**

Your second day in Portland is equally intense. First head to **Speckled Ax** for some early-morning coffee perfection. Then, set a course for **New England Distilling.** Ned Wight, the former head brewer at **Allagash Brewing Company**, owns this distillery and has brought equal skill to his new endeavor. His distillery is just minutes away from his old haunts at Allagash, one of the most influential breweries in New England. This brewery helped to start the wild ale revolution in the United States. Afterward, cross the street to a corporate building that is home to three (yes, three) breweries. If you're still standing, head sixteen miles outside of town to Freeport to **Maine Beer Company** and enjoy one of Maine's most popular but still truly craft breweries.

DAY 5   **Rockin' in Rockland and Rockport**

After enjoying a few days in the city, it's time for country living. Leave Portland and stop at **Oxbow Brewing Company** in Newcastle on your way to the Rockland and Rockport area. Then go to **Sweetgrass Farm Winery & Distillery** in Union. Make extra time at both Oxbow and Sweetgrass, as they're each set in picturesque settings perfect for picnicking and breathing the fresh sea-tinged Maine air. Afterward visit **Rock City Café** and settle down for the night in either Rockland or Rockport.

DAY 6

Whirling in Burlington

The final stop of the tour requires a fair amount of travel. The drive from Rockland/Rockport to Burlington, Vermont is more than five hours by car, but it's worth the trek. In Vermont, beer and beer-like beverages are king, and you'll want to make sure to pay homage to the crown while in Burlington. Get warmed up at **Citizen Cider**, one of the nation's best cider houses. Then walk around the corner to **Maglianero Café**, a top-tier coffeehouse with impeccable pour-overs. Swing over to **Four Quarters Brewing** in nearby Winooski, then head to **Groennfell Meadery** about two and a half miles away in Colchester. Afterward go to downtown Burlington and explore Church Street. Traffic is closed to cars at this outdoor mall, where you can enjoy another great cup of coffee at **Uncommon Grounds Coffee and Tea**. You can cap off your evening with a visit to **The Farmhouse Tap & Grill**, where **Hill Farmstead Beer** is an on-tap staple.

DAY 7

Shake, Brattle, and Roll

God may have rested on the seventh day, but you're not quite done. For the final day of this weeklong extravaganza, you have two choices. You can swing 150 miles south to Brattleboro, or head about 90 miles southeast to the Quechee area. In Quechee, the craft beverage scene is anchored by **Long Trail Brewing Company and Vermont Spirits**. There are also great outdoor attractions, with plenty of hiking options in the warmer months and skiing spots in the winter. Brattleboro is a small but classic Vermont town that is home to **Hermit Thrush Brewery, Saxtons River Distillery,** and **Mocha Joe's Roasting Company,** all within close proximity to one another. Each destination is a winning one and an awesome cap to the week. Choose one for this trip and plan the other for the future, or better yet, add a day or two to your trip.

Suggested Itineraries

The Places

Vermont

Citizen Cider
Maglianero Café
Four Quarters Brewing
Groennfell Meadery
Uncommon Grounds
Coffee and Tea
The Farmhouse
Tap & Grill
Hill Farmstead Brewery
Long Trail Brewing Co.
and Vermont Spirits
Hermit Thrush Brewery
Saxtons River Distillery
Mocha Joe's Roasting
Company

Hill Farmstead Brewery/
Bob M. Montgomery
Images

Three-Day Itinerary: Massachusetts and Rhode Island

Massachusetts may not have the same craft-beverage cachet as Maine or Vermont, but New England's most populous state is brimming with craft businesses, from world-famous breweries to elite coffeehouses. Across the border, Rhode Island is something of a latecomer to the beer and spirits world, but in recent years this small state has been making up for lost time. This three-day trip will allow you to get up close and personal with both state's swilling spots.

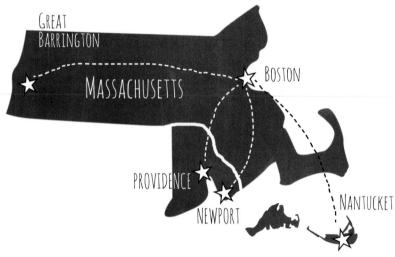

DAY 1 **Harpooned**

Boston is New England's biggest city, and home to one of the region's most-robust craft scenes. Start with a trip to **Harpoon Brewery.** This accessible craft beer giant with a funhouse brewery will appeal to both craft beer nerds and more mainstream beer lovers. From Harpoon go to **Render Coffee,** where you can enjoy one of Boston's best cups of coffee prepared with exacting criteria. Afterward, stop at **GrandTen Distilling.** If you're in the mood for more drinking, visit one of the Boston area's most celebrated smaller breweries, **Trillium Brewing Company.**

DAY 2 — Abby Normal

Start your day at one of **Pavement Coffeehouse's** Boston locations. This local coffee-making institution bridges the gap between specialty and mainstream coffee, keeping coffee nerds and plain old coffee lovers happy. After you're done with your coffee, stop by **Bully Boy Distillers**, then head to **Jack's Abby Brewing.** Jack's Abby recently expanded to feature a 67,000-square-foot space with a sixty-barrel brewhouse at 100 Clinton Street in downtown Framingham. We're confident the beer will be the same quality as at the original brewery. With dozens of different lagers, Jack's Abby is redefining what a lager can be, one delicious brew at a time.

DAY 3 — Riding in Rhode Island

Finish your weekend with a trip to either Providence or Newport. In Providence, you can enjoy drinks from some cutting-edge craft-beverage makers. **Bucket Brewery** is a hip, up-and-coming small brewery with a fun clubhouse-like taproom. **Blue State Coffee** is another excellent coffeehouse with the hot-liquid chops to appeal both to coffee snobs and less-picky coffee drinkers. Alternately, in Newport you can enjoy the boating culture that pervades the waterside city. At **Mokka Coffeehouse** laidback vibes and good coffee is the law of the land. **Newport Storm and Newport Distilling** is a two-for-one brewery and distillery that is one of the first craft alcoholic-beverage producers in modern times to be successful in Rhode Island. Regardless of which city you choose, consider a side trip to **Sons of Liberty Spirits Company**, a craft distillery in South Kingston that is modeled after a brewery and has seasonal whiskeys inspired by various beer styles.

Suggested Itineraries

The Places

Massachusetts
Harpoon Brewery
Render Coffee
GrandTen Distilling
Trillium Brewing Co.
Pavement Coffeehouse
Bully Boy Distillers
Jack's Abby Brewing
Cisco Brewers
Triple Eight Distillery
Fuel Coffee Shop
Berkshire Mountain Distillery
Big Elm Brewing

Rhode Island
Bucket Brewery
Blue State Coffee
Mokka Coffeehouse
Newport Storm & Newport Distilling
Sons of Liberty Spirits Co.

Blue State Coffee

Alternative Massachusetts Trips

TRIP 1

1- to 2-Day: Nothing like Nantucket

A trip to Nantucket often demands a weekend away, since this island requires a ferry ride to reach. After hanging out at one of the beaches, you can enjoy yourself at **Cisco Brewers** and **Triple Eight Distillery**, another two-for-one brewery and distillery that also operates a winery. At this craft-beverage paradise, you can sit outside in the summer and enjoy live music while sampling a variety of craft beers, distilled products, and wines. There are also beer-infused cocktails and food trucks on the premises. What more can you ask for on a warm summer's day?

TRIP 2

1 Day: Beer in the Berkshires

The Berkshire Mountains make for a great day trip but are a bit too far away from Boston to make a visit here a good tie-in with your Boston-area beercation. If you've got time for a side trip or can visit on another weekend, head to Western Massachusetts for what is guaranteed to be a wonderful day of craft beverage tasting. Start your day in downtown Great Barrington at **Fuel Coffee Shop.** After strolling the town with your coffee of choice in hand, head a few minutes outside of town to **Berkshire Mountain Distillery.** You'll quickly learn exactly why this is an award-winning distillery. Across the street is **Big Elm Brewing,** a fun local brewery that is full of heart. Before you leave the area, be sure to stop in at **Bash Bish Falls State Park,** a regional tourist attraction featuring waterfalls and hiking trails, that provides the perfect cap to your visit.

Cisco Breweries

Berkshire Mountain Distillery

Two-Day Itinerary: Connecticut

Connecticut, like Rhode Island, is a latecomer to the world of craft beer and distilleries, but has seen tremendous growth recently. Because of the state's small size, one can get a good sense of the craft-beverage scene without venturing too far off of I-95, making Connecticut the perfect place to explore with a one- or two-day trip.

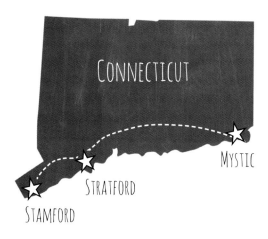

CONNECTICUT

MYSTIC

STRATFORD

STAMFORD

DAY 1 — Into the Mystic

Start your Connecticut adventures with a stop at the classic-style coffeehouse **Green Marble Coffee House,** located in the heart of downtown Mystic, a charming village that is infused with the spirit of sailing and the sea. Just outside this wonderful village you can stop by **Beer'd Brewing Company,** an awesome small brewery that's drawn praise in Connecticut and beyond. The area is also home to **B. F. Clyde's Cider Mill**. The mill is only open in the fall, but if you time your visit correctly, you'll get to see the nation's oldest

Source Coffeehouse

steam-powered cider mill in operation. Travel about sixty-nine miles down I-95 and stop in at Stratford's **Two Roads Brewing Company,** the biggest brewery in Connecticut. After taking the brewery's extensive tour and enjoying some ample sampling, hunker down for the night at the **Inn at Fairfield Beach.**

DAY

2

Half Full of it

Get an early start with an incredible pour-over from **Source Coffeehouse.** Then drive about 20 miles south on I-95. Pull off in Stamford and set a course for **Half Full Brewery,** where you can enjoy accessible, great-tasting craft brews at this brewhouse dedicated to optimism. From there, stop in to recharge at **Lorca Coffeehouse,** an excellent coffeehouse in downtown Stamford. Next, you can swing over the New York border and stop by **StillTheOne Distillery** in Port Chester. While you're in the area you may want to visit **Captain Lawrence Brewing Company** in Elmsford, New York, a well-known Westchester brewery. Afterward, head back to Stamford and catch a show at the **Stamford Center for the Arts.**

Massachusetts

From the charming cobblestone streets of Boston to the beaches of Nantucket, Massachusetts is a state rich with beauty and history. This time around skip the harborside tea party and head straight to the breweries, distilleries, and coffee shops.

Vodka Hearts
Unblended

Bully Boy Distillery

Introduction

Revolution was brewing in Jim Koch's heart.

It was the 1980s, and Koch—like the ringleaders of the American Revolution who had walked Boston's hallowed cobblestone streets centuries before him—was thinking dangerous, radical thoughts. Koch was raging against a foe so fierce, many, including family members, thought he was crazy. He was fighting Big Beer, the powerful mega-breweries like Budweiser, Miller, and Coors. He wasn't just taking on one Goliath; he was David, picking a fight with multiple Goliaths. But unlike craft beer warriors who had come before him, it was a fight that he could win.

In the 1980s, when Koch began to take on Big Beer, the craft-beer movement was still in its infancy, and at any moment, it seemed like it might be snuffed out of existence. Prior to Prohibition, America had a thriving brewing culture with hundreds of breweries, but Prohibition and the culture of mass consumerism that emerged in the United States after World War II took their toll on that tradition. By 1965, Anchor Brewing Company in San Francisco was (according to most modern observers) the only US craft brewery left. That brewery's creative and innovative brews inspired others in the 1970s and '80s, but even though the craft beer movement was growing by the '80s, it was still a fledgling fringe movement, no more of a threat to Big Beer than a ma-and-pa burger joint was to McDonald's. The majority of breweries that did open closed after a few years (including legendary early ones like the New Albion Brewing Company in California), and there were virtually no widely distributed craft brands.

Enter Koch, armed with a double dose of Ivy League degrees (he had both an MBA and a law degree from Harvard) and a family tradition of brewing that went back more than a hundred years. With the mind of a businessman and the heart of an artist, he studied the successes and failures in the craft-brewing industry, and believed that the beer-drinking public was craving something more than the weak lagers widely available. He felt that by combining the fresh ingredients of craft beer with the consistency and quality control of Big Beer, he could take a chunk out of Big Beer's market share. He was right.

Launched in 1984, Koch's Boston Beer Company and its Samuel Adams Boston Lager became a phenomenon. It was the slingshot that demonstrated the Goliaths could be fought successfully. Today, Koch is a billionaire, and his company's beer has become a mainstay in American bars and homes.

While the company's current place in craft-beer circles continues to be debated (some charge it can no longer keep up with the innovation of small and midsize craft breweries), it is undeniable that Boston Beer Company helped to pave the way for the craft industry (both in the brewing and distilling world) by showing that the market share enjoyed by the giants of the industry could be challenged.

The company's small test brewery in Boston offers a free tour that serves as a fun introduction to the brewing world, although it may bore more-experienced liquid vacationers (30 Germania St., Boston; 617-368-5080; samueladams. com). The spirit of revolution successfully fermented by the Boston Beer Company can be found throughout Boston and the state of Massachusetts at large. Currently, innovative breweries in Massachusetts are starting to challenge Maine and Vermont for New England craft-brewing supremacy.

This revolutionary spirit has also spread to the distilling world, which is rapidly expanding in Massachusetts, and has long been present in the coffee culture of the region. It was in Boston that Coffee Connection popularized the notion of single-origin coffee and originated the Frappuccino (later Starbucks purchased it). And the food—well a book could be written on the culinary offerings in Boston, and there probably still wouldn't be enough room to include all of the high-end establishments with superstar chefs and small neighborhood family places with recipes that have stood the test of time.

Traveling the craft-beverage trail of Massachusetts will take you from the rolling mountains of the Berkshires to Boston's city streets to Nantucket, an ocean island of unparalleled beauty that offers a portal to the way things were. The revolution may not be televised, but in Massachusetts it is being brewed with incredible care and skill.

Boston, Part 1

The Trip

There's no better city in which to start your New England craft-beverage adventures than Boston. It was here in this classic Massachusetts metropolis that the American Revolution was born, and where our forefathers showed their preference for coffee by letting the British know just what they could do with their tea.

Part 1 will take a closer look at South Boston, a neighborhood once reeling under the yoke of organized and (equally devastating) disorganized crime, but is now thriving with creativity and all manner of craft-beverage perfection. First we stop at **Harpoon Brewery,** one of the most fun and visitor-friendly breweries in all of New England, and then it's on to **GrandTen Distilling**, an up-and-coming micro-distillery producing powerful spirits. To close the day out we'll visit **Render Coffee,** one of the nation's premier coffee shops.

THE BEER: Harpoon Brewery
306 Northern Ave., Boston
617-456-2322
harpoonbrewery.com

Harpoon is a brewing leviathan and New England craft-beer pioneer that has helped spread the gospel of good beer since it opened in 1986. When Harpoon tapped its first keg, South Boston (or, as the locals call it, "Southie") was a crime-ridden neighborhood under the thumb of gang boss James "Whitey" Bulger. Thanks in part to Harpoon's success and draw, the neighborhood began to transform over the decades. Today, it's a sleek waterside area known as "Sobo" that

Highlights

The Beer
Harpoon Brewery
Located in James "Whitey" Bulger's old stomping grounds.

The Booze
GrandTen Distilling
Inspired by Boston's hard-knocked history. Get the most from your visit on a Friday Night Flights tour.

The Brew
Render Coffee
Most pour-overs are served with a shot of espresso made with the same coffee that was used in the pour-over. Taste the difference.

Harpoon Brewery

is home to almost as many high-end restaurants as Red Sox jerseys.

Though Harpoon beer can be found most anywhere, a trip here is a must for any New England beer pilgrim, as the brewery provides one of the best visitor experiences in the region. As you approach, you see the brightly colored grain tower from a distance. After parking in a garage across the street, you walk in through the taproom. Renovated in recent years, the taproom is a large, open bar that gives you the impression you're standing on the roomy deck of a seagoing vessel. On one side is an expansive view of Southie and the Boston skyline; on the other, the brewery itself.

The company has operated a second brewery in Windsor, Vermont since the early 2000s, but the Boston brewery is the larger Harpoon location and one of the biggest in all of New England. Tours are given multiply times daily and attract large crowds.

The Harpoon tour used to be held on the factory floor, but thanks to recent renovations, tour groups can now travel high above the brewery floor on catwalks specifically designed for observers. This vantage point gives you a bird's-eye view into a truly mammoth brewery full of activity. If visiting during the week, you can see workers hustling to moving cases of bottles and cans off conveyer belts. Watching them work from several stories up gives one the impression of being in a very strange living-art museum.

The best part of the Harpoon tour, like any brew tour, is the tasting. Guests are offered a liberal sampling of "green beer" during the tour, but this is not the St. Patrick's Day variety. In fact, "green" does not refer to the beer's color; rather, it means the beer has not matured and has not been artificially carbonated. Some carbonation occurs naturally during the brewing process, so green beer is not completely flat—just less bubbly than beer that goes to market. While green beer is colder and tastes fresher than the final product, it isn't as refined; drinking it is like grabbing a spoonful of cookie batter. At the end of the tour you are given 20 minutes to have as many samples as you want of finished beer. It's an all-you-can-drink craft-beer buffet.

When the tour is finished, you can hang out in the bar and have one of the brewery's not-to-be-missed pretzels made with by-products of the brewing process. Almost calzone-like in their size and consistency, these pretzels provide the perfect snack.

I found myself hanging in Harpoon's taproom longer than usual following a brewery tour. Sure, it was partly because of the pretzels, but I was also having too much fun to leave. A visit to Harpoon is like a trip to Disneyland, for grown-ups. The staff is sincerely happy, fun, and knowledgeable—like a hipper version of the singing rogues on the Pirates of the Caribbean ride. And believe me, a trip to Harpoon is one ride you won't want to miss.

On Tap

Harpoon has more than twenty varieties of beer available, including a distinct line of unfiltered beers called UFO, which stands for Unfiltered Offering. The brewery also makes a couple varieties of cider, and serious craft-beer drinkers will want to keep an eye on Harpoon's 100 Barrel series, which features limited, one-off releases. Here are some of my favorite Harpoon beers.

Harpooned

Harpoon IPA is a classic example of a New England IPA. First brewed in 1993 as a summer seasonal, it became a year-round offering because of fan demand. It has some hop bite to it, but not so much that it will leave your tongue tingling. This best-selling beer is the flagship of Harpoon's lineup, and it's easy to see why.
ABV: 5.9% | IBUs: 42

Bigger and bolder

Leviathan IPA is a whale of a beer that is big, bold, and in your face (just look at its ABV and IBUs). An Imperial IPA, this beer has an intense flavor and lingering bitterness, and is perfect for hopheads.
ABV: 10.0% | IBUs: 90

U-heF-O

UFO Hefeweizen is an American-style wheat beer that has a cloudy, golden color with a thick, frothy head and a subtle, citrus-like character. It's recommended that the beer is served with a wedge of lemon to complement its fruity, tart fragrance. This beer launched Harpoon's UFO line, and it's clear why the offshoot brand has been so successful. It's a beer I often order when I see it on tap.
ABV: 6.2% | IBUs: 45

THE BOOZE: GrandTen Distilling
383 Dorchester Ave., Boston
617-269-0497
grandten.com

Boston is rich with history, and at **GrandTen Distilling,** the city's ghosts are a constant inspiration. The distillery is in a Dorchester Avenue building that its owners proudly note was a foundry owned by inventor and metallurgist Cyrus Alger in the early 1800s. Firearms were manufactured there, including the first American gun that was ever rifled (grooved in the barrel to stabilize the trajectory of bullets and increase accuracy). "We share our building with the memories of generations of iron workers who forged the tools necessary to build and defend a developing nation," write owners and cousins Matthew Nuernberger and Spencer McMinn on their website. "Although they are now long gone, the brick, mortar, and stout wooden beams remain as a reminder of the hard work and dedication it takes to produce a quality product."

When I catch up with Nuernberger he tells me, "We connect with the idea of the iron foundry, since it was active during the time when manufacturing was the most important industry in America. The products may be different, but we feel the same pride from working hard to create a special product." He says it is not just the foundry that inspires the company, but the neighborhood of South Boston and its history as well. As a result, the distillery features creative spirits as colorful and hard-knuckled as its neighborhood. These include a variety of vodkas and liqueurs powered by everything from almonds to locally grown chipotle peppers to cocoa nibs from an area chocolate factory. GrandTen also produces an Irish whiskey and a variety of gins, including the award-winning **Wire Works American Gin.**

The warehouse-style distillery offers regular tours and tastings, plus a series called Friday Night Flights, a more detailed tour followed by a relaxed tasting of the distillery's full line of products, along with special limited-run spirits not available anywhere else. Nuernberger says the highlight of both tours is how close visitors come to our production process.

"There is nothing separating you from our still, tanks, and equipment," he says. "This gives visitors the chance to see every aspect of what we are doing and how we do it."

Signature Booze

Wire-d

Wire Works is an American gin that . . . well . . . works. It was a triple gold winner at the 2012 MicroLiquor Spirit Awards, and has flavors of spruce tips, kumquat, juniper berry, and angelica root.

Strength: 90 proof

Catch a fire

Fire Puncher Vodka is named for South Boston folk hero Tommy Maguire, who, in 1887 when a fire erupted at the foundry, tried to "fight the flames with his fists" before firefighters arrived. While I can't vouch for the effectiveness of punching flames, this vodka definitely packs a wallop. It's made with heaps of locally grown chipotle peppers, and just before bottling, hickory smoke is bubbled through the spirit for a fiery finish.

Strength: 90 proof

Wearing of the green whiskey

South Boston Irish Whiskey honors the connection between Ireland and Boston with a Boston-made, Irish-style whiskey. The traditional Irish method favors malted barley in the mash bill and copper in the pot still, giving this whiskey a soft, creamy body that will make you want to stand up on your barstool and sing "Danny Boy."

Strength: 80 proof

PLYMOUTH ROCKING

The history of the Boston area, the nation, and, consequently, the world was altered in 1620 because of beer—or rather, a lack thereof. Part of the reason the Pilgrims chose Plymouth Rock as their point of entry into the New World was for the very practical reason that they were running out of beer. By this point, the Pilgrims knew their ship, the *Mayflower*, had ended up well north of its intended destination in Virginia, but with beer supplies running low, they decided to settle in what would become Massachusetts. "We could not now take time for further search or consideration, our victuals being much spent, especially our beere," wrote one member of the voyage. But before you think an intervention and regular AA meetings were in order for the Pilgrims, the beer shortage was more than just a major buzz kill—it was potentially life-threatening. Beer was the primary source of their liquid nourishment, since water would become contaminated on the long transatlantic voyages.

Bar Trivia

THE BREWS: Render Coffee
563 Columbus Ave., Boston
617-262-4142
rendercoffeebar.com

When Chris Dadey opened **Render Coffee,** he didn't want to compromise on quality.

"Before we opened I was a little bit frustrated," Dadey notes. "I was managing cafes, and there were limits to what I could do. My dream was always to open a cafe without those limitations, and basically to do *everything* the right way."

For Dadey, doing everything the right way means preparing each cup of coffee with the proper amount of time and taking the slow-food philosophy to the extreme. Drip coffee is not offered at the cafe, and each pour-over is prepared over the course of four minutes. Taking that much time per cup of coffee was not immediately popular with everyone. "We had a guy storm out the other day yelling, 'God! I just want a large dark roast!' " Dadey told the *Boston Globe* in 2011, shortly after the coffeehouse opened. And that wasn't the worst of it. "Some people flat out told me I was going to go out of business," he recalls.

But Dadey didn't pay attention to the naysayers. Instead, he stuck to what he knew—preparing great coffee—and people quickly came around. Now the open and inviting shop consistently is ranked as one of Boston's best, and often appears on national "best coffeehouse" lists. Locals also fell in love with the place's commitment to quality. "We are kind of like the living room of the south end," Dadey says.

If only my living room served coffee like this. Each pour-over is painstakingly prepared with the type of precision normally not seen outside of labs. The barista pours the coffee into a glass receptacle that is sitting on a digital scale, consults a flow-rate cheat sheet to ensure that the coffee is poured at the proper speed, and times the process to make sure it occurs within the right time frame. "One of the most important parts of a pour-over is controlling all the variables," Dadey says. "You can go to a coffee shop where they're doing pour-overs, but they're not using a scale and they're not using a timer."

The quality of the coffee used is also important. Render uses single-origin grounds from Counter Culture that are based on what's seasonally available. Most pour-overs at Render are served with a shot of espresso made with the same coffee that was used in the pour-over. This allows one to taste the difference between the two styles of coffee presentation.

Beyond pour-overs, Render serves a full line of espresso drinks that also are fueled by single-origin coffee. The coffeehouse offers a variety of pastries and sandwiches, and its bagels, breads, and croissants come from the local bread company, Iggy's Bread, based in Cambridge. It may be secondary to the coffee, but the food is far more than an afterthought, and makes for a tasty breakfast or lunch.

Dadey is dedicated to making coffee right, but he's not one to tell people how to drink it once he gives it to them. "There are some shops in town that don't put out cream or sugar on their condiment bars; I don't really buy into that," he says. "I drink all my coffee black, personally, but people have been putting cream and sugar in their coffee for as long as coffee has been around. I don't feel like it's my position to tell people how to drink it."

Signature Brews

Pour house

As you realize by now, the bread and butter of Render Coffee is its ***pour-overs.*** These specialty drinks are the ones that take four minutes to make and draw die-hard coffee lovers from far and wide. These mugs of perfection are worth the wait.

Cap'n Cino

The ***cappuccino*** is the most popular espresso drink at the cafe. Served according to cappuccino traditions, in a five-ounce cup with two shots of espresso, the result is a strong and powerful beverage with an excellent mix of coffee and foam.

Going hazelnuts

The ***Hazelnut Latte*** is the drink Dadey recommends for specialty-coffee newbies. This delicious concoction is made with roasted hazelnuts pureed with a little sugar and water. Approachable, but still filled with the coffeehouse's signature high-end flavor.

Beyond the Beverages

Where to Eat

Render Coffee sells local baked goods, but if that doesn't do it for you, Harpoon's pretzels are big, doughy, and filling. Those pretzels are the perfect bar food, and if you eat two of them you just might be able to skip dinner. However, if the prospect of stuffing your face with carb-loaded pretzels isn't appealing to you, try the no-nonsense seafood restaurant, **Yankee Lobster Company** (300 Northern Ave., Boston; 617-345-9799; yankeelobstercompany.com), just a few minutes from Harpoon. A few blocks away is **Rosa Mexicano** (155 Seaport Blvd., Boston; 617-476-6122; rosamexicano.com). Skip the entrees—they're good, but not worth the price—and stick to the appetizers. Rosa's famous and one-of-a-kind fresh guacamole and corn tortillas are a treat. There are also great margaritas.

Tapped Out / Where to Stay

Grab a room at **The Westin Boston Waterfront Hotel** (425 Summer St., Boston; 617-532-4600; westinbostonwaterfront.com), or try the swanky **Taj Boston** (15 Arlington St., Boston; 617-536-5700; tajhotels.com).

ROW 34
Photo by Morgan Ione Yeager

Solid Side Trips

If you're in the mood for more drinking, head over to **Row 34** (383 Congress St. in the Fort Point section of South Boston; 617-553-5900; row34.com), a hip oyster bar that is one of the most popular beer destinations in the city and features a rotating lineup of deliciously esoteric beer curated from small and acclaimed breweries throughout the world. To bolster the spirits portion of your trip, stop by **Drink** (348 Congress St., also in the Fort Point section of South Boston; 617-695-1806; drinkfortpoint.com), a highly acclaimed craft cocktail bar where the skilled bartenders will mix drinks based on your preferences.

To keep your liquid vacation copilots happy, stop by the **New England Aquarium** (1 Central Wharf, Boston; 617-973-5200; neaq.org). A great family destination, this South Boston aquarium has a diverse array of wildlife, including turtles, sharks, playful seals, sea lions, and penguins.

The **Boston Children's Museum** (308 Congress St., Boston; 617-426-6500; bostonchildrensmuseum.org) has changing and permanent exhibitions that will keep the younger crowd busy.

For more family fun, or just a chance to relax in the sun while enjoying some cool architecture and getting a taste of local history, stop by **Castle Island** (off William J. Day Blvd., Boston; 617-727-5290). It's a historic South Boston recreation area, and at the park's center is Fort Independence, which once guarded the Pleasure Bay harbor.

Fresh Air

One of the joys of Boston is experiencing it by foot. Harpoon is located in an increasingly hip and upscale South Boston neighborhood. Turn left out of the brewery and follow the water's edge for a scenic South Boston stroll.

The brewery also has easy access to public transportation. The MBTA Silver Line (route SL2) bus stops directly in front of Harpoon Brewery, and can be accessed by taking the Red Line or Commuter Rail to South Station, and then following signs for the Silver Line.

Boston, Part 2

The Trip

For round two of our Boston craft-beverage adventures, Corinne and I headed to **Bully Boy Distillers,** an artisan distillery started by two brothers with farming roots, and then we went to **Pavement Coffeehouse,** a local coffeehouse that also makes bagels. To cap off the experience we traveled a little way outside of Boston to Framingham where **Jack's Abby Brewing,** a brewery that exclusively brews lagers, has been exploding in popularity since it opened in 2011.

 ## THE BEER: Jack's Abby Brewing
100 Clinton St., Framingham
508-872-0900
jacksabby.com

Jack Hendler admits it: The business model for his brewery, Jack's Abby Brewing, has some major flaws.

"On some level it's a pretty stupid business plan," he says while taking a break from conducting tours. But when it comes to craft brewing (and most arts), the line between genius and insanity is pretty thin, and so far Jack's Abby Brewing has managed to walk that line with the grace of a tightrope artist.

The brewery was opened by Jack and his brothers, Eric and Sam. Jack is in charge of brewing and his brothers handle the business end of things. The Hendler brothers wanted to highlight Jack's unique brewing talents, so they decided to exclusively brew German-inspired lagers with American creativity. As beer enthusiasts know, lagers take considerably more time to brew than ales, making them more expensive to produce because they take up valuable barrel space. It takes about a month for Jack's Abby to make each batch of beer—roughly twice as long as it takes most other breweries to make their products.

Jack believes that by brewing lagers, his brewery is able to distinguish itself in the crowded craft-beer market. Jack says, "we think that we can make a better beer with the German brewing process." Far from "stupid," the strategy has ultimately led to more sales, and made the added cost of brewing lagers financially feasible.

Recently after my 2014 visit to Jack's Abby, the brewery announced plans to expand to a 67,000-square-foot space with a sixty-barrel brewhouse at 100 Clinton Street in downtown Framingham. That expansion is now complete. The new facility is almost six times bigger than the original brewery, and has a 5,000-square-foot tasting room and restaurant with traditional German pretzels and other menu items.

Jack studied brewing at the Siebel Institute of Technology World Brewing Academy in Chicago (a brewing school that has been operating in the Windy City since the 1860s), and also studied traditional lager brewing in Munich, Germany.

When Jack and his brothers opened their brewery, they wanted to draw on that German lager brewing knowledge and tradition. Although German brewing is acclaimed the world over and a personal favorite of mine, it's a fairly rigid tradition. In 1516, Bavarian noblemen passed a law known as the Beer Purity Law, or *Reinheitsgebot*, that decreed only water, barley, and hops could be used to brew beer—at the time brewers didn't know that yeast existed. In the five centuries since the law's passage, German brewers, for the most part, have played by the rules. And although Jack is inspired by traditional lager brewing, he is not constrained by it; instead, he strives to combine ancient German brewing expertise and techniques with the experimental try-anything spirit of American craft brewing. The Jack's Abby lineup is full of difficult-to-classify beers, including an **India Pale Lager,** or IPL.

The brewery's name is a play on words: Jack's wife is named Abby, and many of the great lagers in history were brewed by monks who lived and made beer in *abbeys*. The name originated when Jack brewed a batch of beer he called Jack's Abby for the couple's wedding.

Highlights

The Beer
Jack's Abby Brewing
Hard-to-classify (easy to drink) German-inspired lagers.

The Booze
Bully Boy Distillers
Specialties include a fruit-and-spice-infused rum called Hub Punch.

The Brew
Pavement Coffeehouse
Great coffee, a hip atmosphere, and lots of bagels.

Jack's Abby Brewing

Corinne and I visited Jack's Abby early on a Saturday afternoon. It was the final stop on a marathon weekend of brewery tours that included visits to three other breweries and several late-night reunions with friends in the Boston area. Normally my drink of choice on a day like that would have been coffee. However, as soon as I tried the beer at Jack's Abby, all thoughts of switching to a different beverage ceased.

Jack's Abby's motto is "Drink Local, Drink Lager." Living a few hours away from the brewery, I agree with the second part of the slogan, but sometimes have trouble adhering to the "drink local" clause, especially when I see a bottle of Jack's Abby lager for sale.

On Tap

Saying Mass

Mass Rising is a double IPL infused with ever-increasing amounts of American hops during the brewing process. Its aggressive hop-forward flavor is balanced by its lager smoothness and powerful citrus flavor. This widely available beer is every bit as good as some harder to find double IPA offerings.
Availability: Year-round
ABV: 8% IBUs: 100

Framinghammer

Named for the brewery's hometown, this beer is big and bold. An unusual lager style, the beer has many similarities to Imperial Stouts. A lengthy conditioning period creates a silky chocolaty mouth feel enhanced by the use of oats and brown sugar. The beer's noticeable sweetness gets balanced by roasted malt and hop bitterness. With its high alcohol content, it's brewed to keep you warm on cold winter nights.
Availability: Early winter
ABV: 10% IBUs: 55

Saxonator

This beer's name is not, as I initially thought, inspired by a saxophone player who plays a really mean solo; instead it's a nod to German history and the fierce Germanic tribe, the Saxons. Regardless, it is one heck of a beer. It has a full body with raisin-tasting dark fruit, and a slightly roasted and thick malt character. Though full of distinctive flavor, it remains a very palatable beer. Lagered for two months, this slowly brewed beer will make a quick impression on your taste buds.
Availability: Late winter
ABV: 9% IBUs: 25

THE BOOZE: Bully Boy Distillers
35 Cedric St., Boston
617-442-6000
bullyboydistillers.com

When they were kids, brothers Will and Dave Willis discovered a secret room in the basement of their fourth-generation family farmhouse in Sherborn. Inside the room was a fieldstone vault covered in cobwebs and dust and brimming with mystery and allure. Within the vault were Prohibition-era spirits made generations ago by local artisans. Family tradition holds that this subterranean lair was an informal speakeasy for friends and local families, where brands with names like "Medford Rum" and "Cow Whiskey" were drunk and enjoyed. The brothers describe those spirits as harsh and "remarkably undrinkable" today, but still filled with character.

Both that old collection of spirits and life on the family farm were integral inspirations for the brothers, leading to their ultimate decision to create **Bully Boy Distillers** in 2010.

Growing up on the farm, between "baling hay in the summer, chopping wood in the winter, and helping out wherever we could," Will says he and his brother started making cider. "As we got older our interest switched to hard cider, and eventually distilled spirits," he says. "The farm has always been the soul of our family, but it's tough to make farming work in Massachusetts. After college, Dave and I both set off for careers in corporate America. During this time, we were still home-distilling as a hobby, and eventually decided to take a leap of faith and start Bully Boy. From the beginning, Bully Boy Distillers has been a way for us to carry on our family's legacy of local agriculture while paying homage to New England's rich craft-distilling history."

The distillery produces a variety of vodkas, whiskeys, and rums, as well as a fruit-and-spice-infused rum called Hub Punch, a perfect drink for the summer months. Will says the secret to the distillery's sought-after spirits is the flexibility its smaller size affords. "One of the best things about being a small distillery, and really, our biggest competitive advantage, is that we can take chances. For instance, we're doing a lineup of whiskeys based on beer recipes. For the larger distilleries, this might be too outside-the-box to pursue," he explains.

To experience the distillery in person requires coordination and planning. It's open only at the select times listed on the distillery's website. Guests who wish to participate in tours have to make reservations in advance. Although this system eliminates spur-of-the-moment decision-making, it allows for an intimate experience once you've booked a tour. To make visiting even more tricky, there is no signage on the building. So look for a tan warehouse with a "35" on the door and a parking lot in front. If you plan to take a cab home or to your hotel, make sure to call for one since the distillery is in an area where roving cabs are scarce.

When it comes to job roles at the distillery, Will oversees the business side of things while Dave manages all the distilling. But since it's a family affair, both brothers end up doing a little bit of everything—and so do their relatives. "We even enlist our parents and in-laws to help label bottles from time to time," Will says. Together the Willis brothers are keeping the spirit—or, should we say, spirits—of their family farm alive by producing a local artisan product.

Signature Booze

Rum-pelstiltskin

The distillery's signature **White Rum** is aimed at re-creating Boston's legacy as a center of rum production. Made with blackstrap molasses and using techniques handed down from cognac distillers, this rum has depth and a smooth finish, and is perfect for cocktails or enjoying straight.
Strength: 80 proof

Wheat vodka

Bully Boy's USDA-certified organic **White Vodka** is made with a wheat base in a 600-liter copper still. The use of wheat creates a spirit with a subtle sweetness and delicious drinkability. Distilled only once, this vodka has a silky texture and clean finish.
Strength: 80 proof

Punch drunk

Inspired by the original **Hub Punch** recipe popular in the late 1800s, Bully Boy's Hub Punch is a barrel-aged rum infused with fruits and botanicals. Conceived at the defunct Hub Hotel, Hub Punch was enjoyed with soda water, ginger ale, or lemonade. Fittingly, Bully Boy's resurrection of the beverage is fruit-forward, with the botanicals providing tea-like undercurrents of flavor.
Strength: 70 proof

THE BREWS: Pavement Coffeehouse

44 Gainsborough St., Boston (and other locations in Boston)
617-859-7080
pavementcoffeehouse.com

Part cool bagel shop, part high-end specialty coffeehouse, and part neighborhood hangout, **Pavement Coffeehouse** is a local chain of several Boston coffee shops that may not have it all, but comes pretty darn close.

The Pavement Coffeehouse location closest to Bully Boy Distillers is on Gainsborough Street, about two miles away, and the trip takes about twelve minutes by car (Boston has a lot of traffic). The Gainsborough coffeehouse is sleek and modern, with an eclectic youthful vibe and, like all Pavement locations, manages to serve a tremendous number of customers without compromising the coffee.

"We appeal to the coffee geek with a simple menu of excellent single-origin coffees and meticulously prepared espresso beverages," says Wolfie Barn, the company's director of coffee. "But perhaps more importantly, we try to appeal to folks who aren't necessarily already fully initiated coffee geeks. We provide comfortable spaces and delicious signature beverages with house-made ingredients."

That strategy works, and has helped to make the coffeehouse one of the most popular in Boston. Before they are allowed to work the espresso bar, each employee goes through a rigorous training regimen, and must pass the Pavement barista certification exam. But despite Pavement's commitment to quality across the board, the company is all about encouraging differences and creativity at each location.

"All of our locations are designed a little differently," says Marissa Molinaro, the company's director of design and communications. "We're not cookie-cutter people, so we don't want cookie-cutter cafes—although we do like cookies. We encourage our employees to be themselves with discerning, but not rigid, customer service, and that value of authenticity permeates our cafes, from the music we play to the way we talk about coffee."

The food served at Pavement also is top-notch. Company founder Larry Margulies was a bagel shop owner who supplied several local coffeehouses before he went into the coffee business himself. He still takes bagel-making seriously, and a variety of house-made bagels, cream cheeses, and made-to-order breakfast sandwiches are offered.

With great coffee, and lots of bagels, Pavement is a craft-beverage destination worth seeking out in its own right, and definitely worth a visit for recharging between other drinking adventures in Boston.

Pavement Coffeehouse offers a variety of single-origin drip and iced coffees that are always popular and always delicious. Single-origin coffees are used for the cafe drinks. One of the most popular beverages at the coffeehouse—and one you don't want to leave without trying—is the **Spanish Latte.** This enchanting drink is made with a double shot of espresso, a house-made sweetened condensed milk and silky steamed milk, and then served with latte art. It's easy to see why Barn calls it the coffeehouse's "gateway drug."

Thanks a Latte

Pavement Coffeehouse offers a variety of single-origin drip and iced coffees that are always popular and always delicious. Single-origin coffees are used for the cafe drinks. One of the most popular beverages at the coffeehouse— and one you don't want to leave without trying—is the *Spanish Latte*. This enchanting drink is made with a double shot of espresso, a house-made sweetened condensed milk and silky steamed milk, and then served with latte art. It's easy to see why Barn calls it the coffeehouse's "gateway drug."

Bully Boy Distillers
(*page 35*)

Pavement Coffeehouse

Nantucket

The Trip

This Massachusetts island, 30 miles south of Cape Cod, was one of Herman Melville's muses. Though he didn't visit in person until later in life, Nantucket serves as the starting point for the fictional voyage in *Moby Dick*. Visiting this beautiful island you, too, will be inspired—not necessarily inspired enough to write a leviathan-length tale of whaling, morality, and a sea captain with anger-management problems, but inspired nonetheless—especially if you explore the island's wondrous craft-beverage scene.

Nantucket houses **Cisco Brewers** and **Triple Eight Distillery,** an all-in-one brewery, distillery, and wine vineyard that is a powerhouse of craft-beverage production in New England. You can also find **Nantucket Coffee Roasters,** a classic New England roastery that operates an excellent coffeehouse. Visiting both truly is a must for craft-beverage lovers in the area. In warmer months, Cisco/Triple Eight is one of the most fun craft-beverage locales to visit in all of New England. A visit to the island is a perfect day trip during a Cape Cod vacation, and a wonderful weekend getaway in its own right.

Highlights

The Beer
Cisco Brewers
Located on a rolling vineyard that retains its farm-like charm.

The Booze
Triple Eight Distillery
Craft beverage powerhouse is a must-visit 21+ wonderland.

The Brew
Nantucket Coffee Roasters
Enjoy old-school coffee on the cobblestone streets of this historic whaling city.

Cisco Brewers

THE BEER AND THE BOOZE
Cisco Brewers / Triple Eight Distillery
5 Bartlett Farm Road, Nantucket
508-325-5929
ciscobrewers.com

A few minutes before the daily four p.m. tour begins at **Cisco Brewers, Triple Eight Distillery,** and **Nantucket Vineyard** (which are all part of the same company), Jeffrey Horner, the chief brewer and tour guide extraordinaire, arrives, bringing with him a California summer's worth of laid-back vibes. Dressed in shorts and sandals and riding a bicycle, he starts the tour by going to a refrigerator in the brewery and handing out half a dozen growlers filled with Cisco beer. He explains that he talks a lot during the tour, and it can get boring and technical, so he encourages guests to "drink up." And he means it. The amount of "sampling" that takes place on this tour will challenge even experienced craft-beer drinkers.

What follows that announcement is a detailed and informative walk through the different phases of the craft-beverage powerhouse that is Cisco and Triple Eight, a brewery, distillery, and winery all rolled into one real-world paradise of craft beverages.

And it's not just the tour that's great; the setting—outside of downtown Nantucket on the grounds of a rolling vineyard that retains its farm-like charm—is one of the most beautiful you'll have a chance to visit on a craft-beverage tour in New England (or anywhere else in the world, for that matter).

The brewery and distillery are set on a small compound with various buildings that are close together, including an outdoor taproom overlooking the vineyard. There are multiple bars: One specializes in cocktails, one is a wine bar, another offers various Cisco brews on tap, and another one specializes in beer-and-spirit combination cocktails. Crowds flock here, and live bands frequently perform on an outdoor stage during the summer months.

During our visit an excellent reggae band grooved to island classics by Bob Marley, Jimmy Cliff, and other reggae greats—the perfect complement to a relaxed afternoon of craft-beverage drinking. The brewery and distillery remain open and operating during the winter; it's just more fun to visit the place, and the island in general, when it's warm outside.

The beautiful setting would make this a worthwhile destination even if the beer and spirits were simply average, but at Cisco and Triple Eight Distillery, nothing is subpar. The beer is rich and distinctive, the spirits well-crafted and memorable. Beyond Cisco's year-round offerings there is a variety of specialty brews from the brewery's Island Reserve series that includes a delectable barley wine, full-throttled Double IPA, and distinctive Gose (a traditional tart and salt-flavored style of beer).

Because of the huge shipping costs associated with brewing on an island, Cisco contract brews much of its beer at F. X. Matt Brewing Company in Utica, New York, a well known contract brewery that also brews the majority of Brooklyn Brewery's beer and produces Costco's Kirkland beer. Unlike other breweries where it's hard to tell what is brewed where, Cisco makes it clear: All Island Reserve products are brewed on the island and all others are brewed at F. X. Matt in accordance with Horner's specifications.

As for spirits, Triple Eight Distillery creates a variety of high-end beverages all powered by Nantucket's freshwater supply. Highlights of the Triple Eight Distillery include Gale Force Gin, Hurricane Rum, and the Notch, or "Not Scotch," a New World whiskey.

While wine is one of the few alcohol-powered beverages that falls outside the scope of this book, I couldn't resist indulging in a few samples. My favorite was the impressively labeled and tasty Nantucket Vineyard 2009 port.

On Tap

Going Grey

A unique and refreshing wheat beer, *Grey Lady* is named for the often-foggy island of Nantucket. This wheat beer is fermented with Belgian yeast and has hints of tropical fruit. The result is a bold and spicy beer that is the type of drink you're either going to love or hate. I love it, and it's one of a select few beers that almost always has a spot in my fridge.
ABV: 4.5%

Tall tales

The flagship of Cisco Brewery is *Whale's Tale Pale Ale,* an English-style pale ale with an excellent balance of hop bitterness. This is probably the Cisco brew you're most likely to encounter at a beer bar or liquor store outside of Massachusetts, and there's a reason for that: It's excellent.
ABV: 5.5%

Taller tales

Cisco ups the ante from its pale ale with its robust *India Pale Ale.* There's a higher alcohol content, more hop bitterness, and bigger, bolder flavor.
ABV: 6.5%

Signature Booze

Rock you like a hurricane

Nantucket's hurricane season is the inspiration behind *Hurricane Rum,* a high 88.8-proof rum whose strength was designed to reflect the awesome and terrifying natural power of a hurricane. Aged in bourbon casks, this rum has a golden color and hints of caramel and vanilla, along with a smoky tobacco flavor.

Strength: 88.8 proof

Voting for vodka

The distillery's flagship product, *Triple 8 Vodka,* is triple-distilled from organically grown grain and then blended with the distillery's exceptionally clean and soft water drawn from well No. 888 (the inspiration for the distillery's name). For three years in a row (2003–05) Triple 8 Vodka outscored the Netherlands' vodka super-distillery Ketel One in the World Spirits Competition conducted by the Beverage Testing Institute.

Strength: 80 proof

Not scotch

Since spirits produced outside of Scotland cannot be called scotch, Triple Eight decided to call its scotch-like spirit *Notch*—short for "not scotch." Thanks to Nantucket's Scotland-esque climate (moderate temperatures, lots of fog), this "not scotch" has a distinctly scotch-like flavor. The single-malt New World whiskey is distilled from pure glacier water and aged for eight years. First it spends several years in American white-oak casks, and then for its final months, it's transferred to Nantucket Vineyard's French oak merlot-soaked casks, which imbues the Notch with its red hue.

Strength: 90 proof

THE BREWS: Nantucket Coffee Roasters / The Bean Coffee Shop

4 India St., Nantucket
508-228-6862
nantucketcoffee.com

Long before it was the domain of beret-wearing hipsters with mustaches and beards, artisan coffee was made by hearty, old-school New Englanders. Great coffeehouses were ma-and-pa operations, and coffee was the down-to-earth drink of no-nonsense people who took great pride in what they brewed and crafted it with skill. So it's fitting that on Nantucket, an island rich with history, you can find exactly this type of throwback coffeehouse at **The Bean Coffee Shop,** owned and operated by **Nantucket Coffee Roasters,** which distributes its specialty-roasted coffee beans across the country.

Nantucket Coffee Roasters produces a variety of organic coffee blends and rum- and whiskey-barrel-aged coffee beans. You can order these roasts from the website or enjoy a well-prepared cup of coffee there. This quaint coffeehouse is inside a small building that has a couple of other stores, like a mini mall. You won't find pour-overs or other more modern coffee-shop concoctions here; instead, you'll find the basics, done exceptionally well—a regular coffee, black or with cream; refreshing iced coffee; and excellent lattes and cappuccinos.

The magic of each of these drinks begins in the roaster, explains Monique Harrington, office manager for both Nantucket Coffee Roasters and The Bean Coffee Shop. "There is no automation involved in our process," she says. "We do a good amount of aroma-roasting with our beans. Every batch of coffee is roasted by hand and carefully controlled by our roaster to bring out the best characteristics of each varietal bean."

There is also great attention to detail, including from how we clean the machines, how we dump the drip coffee sitting for longer than twenty minutes, the multiple coffee bean options, how the coffee is roasted, to the intricacy of how we pull our shots that make the difference. You can go anywhere on the island for 'a cup of plain old coffee.' But if you truly care about the quality, we are the place."

The roastery was opened in 1993 by coffee aficionado Wesley Van Cott. Seven years later The Bean was opened to showcase the specialty coffees being roasted. Enjoying this old-school coffee on the cobblestone streets of this historic whaling city is a not-to-be-missed treat.

Signature Brews

The people's choice

One of the most popular roasts at The Bean is the *Café Blend,* a clean, crisp blend with hints of chocolate and fragrant fruit that straddles the tasting line between medium and full-bodied. This is the go-to, must-try roast at The Bean, and it does not disappoint.

Season's brewings

Another concoction to seek out here is any of the always-popular specialty seasonal drinks. In the fall these include the *Great Harvest Latte* and the hot mulled and chai cider.

Boozers

The blends are part of the roastery's *Boozy Beans* series, including the *Rum Cask Conditioned Ethiopian Yirgacheffe* and the *Whisky Barrel Conditioned Ethiopian Yirgacheffe.* These beans do not actually have alcohol in them, but they are infused with alcohol flavors after being aged for thirty days in rum and whiskey barrels from the Triple Eight Distillery.

Bar Trivia

Vodka Neutrality

Vodka has some unusual characteristics. First, unlike most other spirits, it is not defined by the ingredients with which it is made; instead, it is classified based on what it becomes. So you can use honey, molasses, corn, rye, grapes, and even potatoes to start with, and as long as the finished product is distilled at 190 degrees and is bottled at 80 proof or above, it can be called vodka.

Second, the best non-flavored vodka essentially is supposed to be tasteless. According to its official US definition, it is "a neutral spirit" without "distinctive character, aroma, taste, or color." As baseball legend Yogi Berra might say, "If the vodka tastes great, it's probably bad."

Beyond the Beverages

Where to Eat

Given the beauty of the setting and quality of the alcohol offered, once you stop by Cisco Brewers / Triple Eight Distillery, you may never want to leave. The good news is, you don't have to. There are a variety of food trucks on the premises during peak times that should satisfy any food cravings.

In addition, the downtown has plenty of options from which to choose. If flavor, not ambience, is what you seek, skip downtown and head for the local seafood joint, **Sayle's Seafood** (99 Washington St. Ext., Nantucket; 508-228-4599; saylesseafood.com). This place has great lobsters, fried clams, clam chowder, and just about every sea-caught delicacy you'd want to sink your teeth into while visiting a seafaring town.

For dessert try the **Juice Bar** (12 Broad St., Nantucket; 508-228-5799). Don't be fooled by the health-club-sounding name; just a few blocks away from the harbor and main ferry terminal, this island favorite specializes in ice cream. Known for homemade warm, crumbly, cookie-like waffle cones, this shop is beloved. Lines sometimes wrap around the block during the busy season, but it's worth the wait if you have the time.

Tapped Out / Where to Stay

There's no getting around it: Staying the night in Nantucket during the summer is expensive. It also happens to be the best time to visit the island. The **Brass Lantern Inn** (11 North Water St., Nantucket; 508-228-4064; brasslanternnantucket.com) is a more "moderately" priced inn, but still will require you to part with some cheddar. Another option is

Fresh Air

Bringing a car to Nantucket is expensive and unnecessary. Despite being a "small" island, it's still too big to get around solely on foot, but there are plenty of cabs, including **Milestone Taxi** (508-325-5511; milestonetaxi.com). Cisco also runs a regular shuttle from downtown to the brewery, and there are city shuttles with minimal fares from downtown to the beach. A third option is to explore the island on a bicycle. Bike rental companies include **Young's Bicycle Shop** (508-228-1151; youngsbicycleshop.com).

Brass Lantern Inn
Photo by Jumping Rocks

Nantucket Inn (1 Miller Ln., Nantucket; 508-228-6900; nantucketinn.net), which often has the most affordable rooms on the island but still charges more than you'd pay for the same room on the mainland.

A third option, and the one I generally favor, is to make Nantucket a day trip. The traditional ferry trip from Hyannis on Cape Cod takes about two hours, but for an extra $30 or so per person, a high-speed ferry cuts the trip down to an hour (it's also a more enjoyable voyage). The high-speed ferry makes visiting Nantucket and visiting its beaches and craft-beverage scene in a single day a more-viable option. Doing it this way, you can spend the night in Hyannis, where it's easier to find more reasonably priced rooms. Two separate companies run traditional and high-speed ferries between Hyannis and Nantucket (hylinecruises.com; steamshipauthority.com); check their websites for schedules and fares.

Solid Side Trips

Cisco Brewery takes its name from **Cisco Beach** on Hummock Pond Road, a beautiful and secluded beach that is a favorite of surfers and locals. It has big waves, but also often has strong rip currents. The more swimmer-friendly beach is **Surfside** at the end of Surfside Road (keeping going until you see the waves). You can get here via a three-mile bike path or by jumping on the regularly scheduled downtown shuttle. This beautiful beach is usually more crowded than Cisco, but has changing rooms and bathrooms.

Surfside is wide and long, and although it's not the top surfer destination on Nantucket, the waves can be intense. During a family vacation in my youth, my little brother Levon was pushed so hard into the sand that he looked like a sandman. During my research trip to Nantucket, Corinne caught a wave and gashed her arm when it body-slammed her into the ground (liquid vacationing comes with its scars).

Beyond the beaches, downtown Nantucket is to history lovers what Cisco Brewery / Triple Eight Distillery is to craft beverages—there's so much to take in that it's almost overwhelming. A personal favorite is the **Whaling Museum** (13 Broad St., Nantucket; 508-228-1894; nha.org).

Great Barrington & Sheffield

The Trip

Almost equidistant from Boston and New York City, the Great Barrington area is a *great* day-trip option for New Yorkers or Bostonians looking to escape the big city and enjoy a country town with a metropolitan flair. Guests can shop along the main street, enjoy nearby natural wonders such as **Bash Bish Falls State Park** or **Monument Mountain,** and soak up lots of craft-beverage excellence.

I was drawn to the area after reading some articles that heaped well-deserved praise on **Berkshire Mountain Distillery,** a short drive from downtown Great Barrington in neighboring Sheffield. As I learned more about the area, I was delighted to discover the distillery is next to the up-and-coming Massachusetts craft brewery, **Big Elm Brewing.** During a wonderful day trip in the fall of 2014, Corinne and I stopped at **Fuel Coffee Shop,** a beloved downtown Great Barrington coffeehouse, sampled local cuisine and nature trails, and then visited Berkshire Mountain and Big Elm for an excellent afternoon. We capped off the epic day with a trip to the **Barrington Brewery and Restaurant.**

THE BEER: Big Elm Brewing
65 Silver St., Sheffield
413-229-2348
bigelmbeer.com

In the early 2000s, the Victory Brewing Company in Downingtown, Pennsylvania, was alive with yeast strains, the smell of hops, and romance—at least for young beer enthusiasts Christine and Bill Heaton. The

Highlights

The Beer
Big Elm Brewing
Beer that appeals to all, from a American lager to a tasty saison to a milky stout.

The Booze
Berkshire Mountain Distillery
Famous for Greylock Gin, named #1 craft gin by *The New York Times.*

The Brew
Fuel Coffee Shop
Delightfully cluttered quintessential New England coffee shop.

Big Elm Brewing

two met while working there, fell in love, married, and did what most newly-weds do: open a brew pub.

That brew pub, **Pittsfield Brew Works** in Pittsfield, Massachusetts, which the couple took over in 2005, was successful in some ways, but running the business was different than the Heatons expected. "What we know and love is making beer, which became only a side task of running the brew pub," Christine explains.

So in 2010, soon after their first son was born, they sold the brew pub and began the planning a production brewery. Finding a suitable location proved tricky, but a few years ago they found their current space in Sheffield, and everything fell into place.

The brewery opened in the fall of 2013 and has become a craft-beer oasis in the Berkshire Mountains. It is named for Sheffield's "big elm," a historic elm tree whose image adorns the town's seal and grew for four hundred years—just yards away from where the brewery now sits—before it was cut down in the 1920s. The tree once served as a community gathering place, and it was said that nearly five hundred people could fit under its sprawling canopy. The tree may be long gone, but the community spirit it fostered is alive and well at **Big Elm Brewing**.

There was a mix of tourists and locals alike congregating in the taproom when Corinne and I stopped in on an autumn Saturday. Many of the guests, like us, had wandered over following a visit to **Berkshire Mountain Distillers,** which is across the street within easy walking distance. The bright and open taproom overlooks the brewery through a small door. Christine was on hand, enthusiastically explaining the brewing process of each beer and the backstory of the brewery.

Both Christine and her husband entered the brewing business through unconventional routes. Bill, a photographer, grew tired of wedding and advertising photography and took an entry-level job cleaning kegs at Victory Brewing, where he worked his way up the ladder. Christine was a chemistry major at Millersville University, Pennsylvania when she became intrigued by home brewing. After a stint in the Peace Corps, she decided to break into the "boys' club" of the brewing industry. Along the way she studied brewing at the Siebel Institute's Doemens Academy in Munich, Germany.

Big Elm's beers brewed at the couple's brewery have craft-beer complexity but are approachable. Ranging from a hoppy IPA to an easy-drinking American lager, from a tasty saison to a milk stout, there's something that will appeal to almost every beer taste. While there's no telling if the brewery will survive the four hundred years its namesake tree did, the place is establishing some pretty deep brewing roots.

On Tap

True IPA
The **Big Elm IPA** is an American IPA in the classic sense of the style, with big assertive hop flavors up front. Though bitter, it still has a rich complexity of flavors that will make you come back for seconds.
ABV: 7%

Reppin' the 413
The **413 Farmhouse Ale** is the brewery's take on the classic farmhouse ales of Belgium, and you'll want to take a growler or two of this home with you. Brewed with choice barley, wheat malt, and local honey from Bear Meadow Apiary, this beer is refreshing and full of flavor.
ABV: 6%

Dog-day afternoon
Named for the brewery's mascot, aka the family dog, the **Gerry Dog Stout** is an oatmeal stout made with choice American and English barley, rolled oats, and herbal American hops. The result is rich velvety goodness.
ABV: 6.5%

She-Brew

Female brewers like Christine Heaton are less common today than their male counterparts, but that was not always the case. In ancient Mesopotamia and Egypt, where Western beer was born, brewing was primarily, but not exclusively, done by the women, who also made bread as part of their household duties. The Code of Hammurabi, one of the world's earliest written laws, spelled out strict penalties for brewers who overcharged for their beer. In Egypt, beer was part of the pharaoh's daily diet, and hieroglyphics and pictures in tombs depict early women brewers.

Bar Trivia

THE BOOZE: Berkshire Mountain Distillers
356 South Main St., Sheffield
413-229-0219
berkshiremountaindistillers.com

The water from mountain springs known as Berkshire Sodium Springs was so good, it became a tourist attraction. A hotel opened up in the 1800s so wealthy New Yorkers could swim in the water and cure what ailed them. The hotel burned down in the 1900s, but the springwater was later bottled and sold as a cure-all. In 1901, the *Pittsfield* (Massachusetts) *Sun* declared the waters the finest in the world.

Today that water provides the backbone of all the spirits produced by **Berkshire Mountain Distillers.** While a sip of one of these products won't necessarily provide a miracle cure, it will give distillery lovers a chance to taste some of the best and most celebrated spirits produced in New England. The distillery's **Greylock Gin** was named the number-one craft gin in America by the *New York Times* in 2012, and the company has worked with Massachusetts legend Jim Koch, founder of Samuel Adams, on a variety of whiskey collaborations, including a whiskey that uses Samuel Adams Boston lager. The distillery also produces vodka, rum, and a variety of bourbons and other whiskeys.

Each product I tried during my visit was excellent. Besides Samuel Adams, the distillery also works with other craft breweries to age its bourbon in recently used beer barrels. These breweries include local ones like **Big Elm Brewing** (across the street) and national ones like New York's **Brewery Ommegang** and Michigan's **Founders Brewing.**

A stop to the visitor-friendly distillery is a must for any Massachusetts liquid vacationer. The large tasting room often is crowded on weekends, especially during leaf-peeping season, but the staff makes sure everyone gets a sample and takes time to explain each product. There are formal tours and tastings that can be scheduled in advance, but guests who don't plan ahead can stop in for informal self-guided tours.

Founder Chris Weld credits a large part of the distillery's success to the water from that legendary spring, located on the farm he and his wife purchased in 2007. "The waters are granite-based and add a wonderful natural viscosity and sweetness to our spirits," he says.

Water is the basis of any good spirit, or beer, for that matter, but it's not the only thing owners of a successful spirit company need. They also must have recipes and a passion for what they do. Developing recipes is a trial-and-error process that can be a little like prospecting for gold, For instance, the recipe for the award-winning Greylock Gin, which features seven high-quality botanicals, was discovered after "countless test batches." Weld recalls, "One day one of the recipes just hit—it was a eureka moment."

As for the passion part of the equation, Weld has had that for a long time. His interest in distillation was first inspired by a book he read on homesteading. He was drawn to the craft because it was an amalgamation of his interest in cooking, science, and agriculture. But when he undertook his first distillation project at home, there was one big problem: He was only fourteen. Although he initially convinced his mother to allow him to continue with the project as part of an eighth-grade class assignment, she put a stop to it when she realized making distilled spirits was a federal offense.

Weld, who grew up in Westchester County, New York, became a physician's assistant and worked in emergency medicine in the San Francisco Bay area. He and his family ultimately moved back to the East Coast and purchased the neglected apple farm. As they cultivated the trees, they tasted the water, and the idea of opening a distillery began to take shape. The distillery became official in 2007, and once again people come from far and wide to taste the waters of that Berkshire mountain spring.

Berkshire Mountain Distillers

Signature Booze

Going Greylock

As mentioned previously, *Greylock Gin* is an award-winning spirit that was named the number-one craft gin in the country by the *New York Times*. While you may or may not agree with that designation, most will agree this is a great gin. Made with seven different botanicals, it starts floral and dry and finishes with strong notes of juniper, achieving the right balance of floral sweetness and alcohol bite.

Strength: 80 proof

Mountain bourbon

The *Berkshire Bourbon* uses corn that comes from a farm just a few miles from the distillery. Smooth and balanced, it has notes of spicy rye, vanilla, and fruit. This spirit also serves as the basis for the distillery's craft-brewery collaboration, where the bourbon is finished within a recently used craft beer barrel.

Strength: 86 proof

Coming 'round the mountain

Ragged Mountain Rum is made with a traditional pot-still method and crafted in small batches. It is aged in oak barrels at high proof before it is blended with water from the distillery's famous well and brought down to its intended proof. Intense and smoky, it's an excellent rum for sipping or mixing.

Strength: 80 proof

You should also try . . .

. . . the bottled **Greylock Gin and Tonic,** a wonderful concoction that allows you to keep what amounts to a superb craft-cocktail bar in your fridge. This 26.6-proof drink is an excellent choice for those of us who are not skilled mixologists. As of early 2015, it was only available in Massachusetts, Connecticut, New York, New Jersey, and Georgia, but I expect distribution to grow.

Moby Dick's Non-Water Birth

Bar Trivia

Although Nantucket (which we visit in the previous chapter) served as one of the early settings in Herman Melville's *Moby Dick*, Great Barrington, located far from the sea, arguably deserves more credit for the finished book. It was while hiking in 1850 at Monument Mountain in Great Barrington with friends from the publishing world that Melville first met Nathaniel Hawthorne. The two writers became friends, and Melville's talks with Hawthorne, who was fourteen years his senior, helped him work out some of the issues he was encountering while writing *Moby Dick*. Ultimately, Melville dedicated his epic work to Hawthorne.

THE BREWS: Fuel Coffee Shop
286 Main St., Great Barrington
413-528-5505
fuelgreatbarrington.com

It was a pleasant cafe, warm and clean and friendly, and I hung up my old water-proof on the coat rack to dry and put my worn and weathered felt hat on the rack above the bench and ordered a café au lait. The waiter brought it and I took out a notebook from the pocket of the coat and a pencil and started to write.

—Ernest Hemingway

So reads the opening quote in the "About Us" section on this coffeehouse's website, which paints you an accurate picture of what to expect: This is a beautiful, quintessential coffee shop in a beautiful, quintessential New England town. It's also the type of place where you'd like to grab a coffee and then sit back with your notebook or laptop to do your best Hemingway impression as you try to write the great American novel or travelogue (you're reading my efforts now).

Corinne and I wandered into this downtown coffee shop at the beginning of our craft-beverage adventures in the area. It's a long and narrow space, filled with the usual coffeehouse suspects—writers/students/artists on laptops, old friends chatting over lattes, and just your everyday quick-and-convenient-coffee-on-my-way-to-wherever crowd. There's a relaxed throwback '90s vibe to the place. Instead of the sparsely decorated and polished wood motif in vogue with many new coffeehouses, **Fuel Coffee Shop** has that delightfully crowded, cluttered feel—the counters overflowing with pastries and menu items, the place vibrant and alive. The bulletin board is crowded with flyers, a sign that the establishment supports the local community by providing a promotional venue for local artists and performers.

Like the ambience, the coffee beverages are old-school but solid. Good drip and iced coffees are available, along with classic espresso-bar favorites like cappuccino, lattes, etc. They're not trying to revolutionize the way coffee is brewed here, and there's nothing wrong with that; this place does what it does well.

Whether you visit at the start of your craft-beverage adventure in Great Barrington or after a long day of beer and spirit sampling, Fuel Coffee Shop is sure to provide fuel for your musings, trips, and explorations of the area.

Signature Brews

E.T., foam home

The *cappuccino* at Fuel is exactly what you'd want and expect from a good cappuccino. It's on the foamy side, with some dark-roast bitterness that is less intense than some artisan espresso-blend offerings.

Ice 'em

In summer and early fall there's no better traveling companion (apologies to my wife) on the streets of Great Barrington than a to-go cup of Fuel's *iced coffee.* It is velvety and refreshing the way iced coffee is supposed to be.

Oh so smoothie

Fuel also offers a good selection of teas and smoothies. I recommend trying a smoothie, in particular the *Wired Monkey,* which features frozen banana, maple syrup, milk, and espresso. It's a coffee-and-fruit concoction that is the answer to your sweet-tooth-espresso prayers.

Beyond the Beverages

Where to Eat

There are good options along Great Barrington's main drag, but craft-beverage lovers may want to drive a few minutes away to grab lunch or dinner at the **Barrington Brewery and Restaurant** (420 Stockbridge Road, Great Barrington; 413-528-8282; barringtonbrewery.net). This brew pub and restaurant brews its beers using solar-powered brewing equipment. Despite this impressive and progressive technique, the brew pub has a rustic Vermont-style charm to it. Mugs hang from the ceiling, families gather for lunch and dinner at big tables, and the beer is hearty and potent in a uniquely New England way. The full menu offers a wide selection of solid bar food, from nachos to burgers. If you've had enough beer for the moment, consider going to **Baba Louie's** (286 Main St., Great Barrington; 413-528-8100; babalouiespizza.com). This artisan restaurant specializes in wood-fired pizza with sourdough bread.

Tapped Out / Where to Stay

If you decide to spend the night, nearby options include **Holiday Inn Express & Suites Great Barrington** (415 Stockbridge Road., Great Barrington; 413-528-1810; ihg.com) or **Fairfield Inn & Suites Lenox Great Barrington** (249 Stockbridge Road, Rte. 7, Great Barrington: 413-644-3200; marriott.com).

Fresh Air

Rural Massachsetts doesn't have reliable public transportation, so you may need to call a cab. Local cab companies include the **Taxi Company of Great Barrington** (413-528-0911).

If you're looking for a great walk, head to **Bash Bish Falls State Park.** This regional tourist attraction offers a moderate forest trail that culminates with a spectacular view of the sixty-foot falls (3 East St., Mount Washington; 413-528-0330).

Another nearby option is **Monument Mountain** (Rte. 7, Great Barrington; 413-298-3239; thetrustees.org/places-to-visit/berkshires/monument-mountain.html). Here a somewhat strenuous walk brings you to the 1,642-foot summit of Squaw Peak for breathtaking views of Mount Greylock near the Vermont border and the Catskill Mountains of New York to the west. You may even spy a hawk overhead or a bald eagle. A walk here helped to inspire the great literary work *Moby Dick*. To get to Monument Mountain from downtown Great Barrington, follow Route 7 north for four miles to the entrance on the left.

Solid Side Trips

During a trip to the area you may want to make time to visit Great Barrington's small but charming downtown. There is pleasant architecture and plenty of shopping options. Speaking of shopping, a few miles from downtown is Asian art imports superstore, **Asia-Barong** (199 Stockbridge Road, Great Barrington; 413-528-5091; asiabarong.com), which is billed as the "largest Asian store in America." Walking into this warehouse-size shop is like stepping onto the set of an awesome kung fu film—there are masks, sculptures, cycle rickshaws, and more. I'm not usually one for shopping excursions while there are beverages to be drunk, but this is an exception. If the book you're now reading becomes a bestseller, I'll be furnishing my mansion with items bought here.

Bonus Brewery

Wachusett Brewing Company
175 State Road East, Westminster
978-874-9965
wachusettbrew.com

As you may have noticed on your own travels, many breweries are found a bit off the beaten path, but **Wachusett Brewing Company** is even farther afield than most.

As you approach this brewery, you'll pass under the shade of evergreens and glimpse bodies of water through the trees. As civilization begins to recede, you'll find the brewery on a quiet stretch of road. Although its standard office-building exterior is not much to look at, it is nonetheless a beacon of brewing quality in the wilderness.

Founded in 1993, Wachusett Brewing Company is ancient in American brewery years, and was an early pioneer in the New England craft-beer movement. Founders Peter Quinn, Ned LaFortune, and Kevin Buckler became friends while all three were attending nearby Worcester Polytechnic Institute. They were brought together because of a shared love of beer and the outdoors.

Armed with technical know-how, passion for beer, and a never-say-never attitude, the three beer lovers left their careers in engineering and biology to open the brewery.

The brewery's first beer, **Wachusett Country Pale,** was released in 1994 and the crisp, distinctive pale ale quickly became a local favorite. In 2001, the brewery began brewing its **Blueberry Ale.** The subtly blueberry-flavored brew would soon become a phenomenon in Massachusetts and New England. Many bartenders would put fresh blueberries in the glass before serving the beer, which added to its mystique.

In the last decade, the brewery has added some other fruit-powered beers to the lineup, including the **Strawberry White,** a traditional Belgian ale complemented by the addition of fresh strawberries. In addition to these sweet beers, Wachusett has a diverse lineup of IPAs that will keep the hopheads hopping, including the delicious **Larry IPA** and the Boston Red Sox-inspired **Green Monsta IPA.**

There is a crammed (in a good way) wild-submarine, steam-punk-laboratory feel to the actual brewing space.

"The owners are engineers," Kim Slayton, the brewery's publicist, says by way of explanation as she leads a small tour group through the maze-like subterranean pathways of unusual-looking brewing equipment.

Slayton explains that much of the equipment was bought secondhand from non-beer industries and modified for the brewing process. The mash tun (where the starches in crushed grains are converted into sugars for fermentation) is an old Louisiana shrimp tank; the fermenters are old dairy tanks; and the can filler used for the brewery's canning line was originally used at a Coca-Cola factory in Bermuda in the 1960s.

When demand for Wachusett Brewing Company beers increased, the brewery needed more space. LaFortune and company decided to expand upward and build a second level. Having two levels with relatively short ceilings makes the brewery less open and expansive than most other breweries, but it also makes it more intriguing.

In addition to its unique visual characteristics, Wachusett Brewing Company is an interesting brewery to visit because it is often the scene of constant activity. It is home to one of the biggest canning lines east of the Mississippi. When the canning line is in operation, the place is full of hustle and bustle, and there's a din as hundreds of cans are filled and capped per hour. These sights, and the beer itself, make this a brewery worth seeking out.

On Tap

Country ale

Country Pale Ale is the first beer brewed by Wachusett Brewing Company. It's also the ale that launched a thousand shipments, and, in so doing, helped engrain the craft-beer revolution in the mountains of Massachusetts. It remains a powerful pale ale with a good balance of hop and malt that will definitely help you get your country groove on.

ABV: 5.1% IBUs: 17

In my blueberry heaven

Mention the Wachusett Brewing Company to someone from Massachusetts and the words you're most likely to hear next are **Blueberry Ale.** This is the beer that put the brewery on the map outside of Massachusetts.

An early entrant into an increasingly popular beer style, Wachusett's Blueberry Ale provides a slight aroma and flavor of blueberry that comes from blueberry extract fermented into a wheat ale base.

ABV: 4.5% IBUs: 10

Lovin' Larry

The **Larry IPA** is my favorite beer in the Wachusett lineup, a double IPA that is loaded with hop power. Despite this beer's high IBU rating, it's not noticeably more bitter than most other IPAs. In fact, the citrus and floral notes of the beer make it extremely drinkable, and give this beer a sensitive side. It's hoppy but full of distinct flavor, and its high alcohol content will get the party started in no time.

ABV: 8.5% IBUs: 85

Lagers vs. Ales

Generally speaking, all beers are either ales or lagers, although there are subcategories of both. Ales are brewed using top-fermenting yeast while lagers are brewed with bottom-fermenting yeast, and lagers are brewed at cooler temperatures than ales. In layman's terms, the biggest difference is that the brewing process takes much longer with lagers. The word *lager* comes from the German word *lagern*, which means "to store," and refers to the "lagering" process in which the beer is stored for long periods of time. The two different brewing techniques also create distinct flavor profiles. Because of their warmer fermentation temperatures, ales usually contain a range of spicy and fruity flavors derived from the yeast during the brewing process. Ale recipes also tend to contain more malt and hops, producing more-bitter, cloudier beers. In contrast, as a result of their cool-fermenting yeast strains, lagers have less yeast-derived flavors than ales; they also offer a clearer expression of grains and hops, and a smoother, cleaner taste that can be more palatable for those who shy away from bitter beer.

Bar Trivia

Another Round: Massachusetts

Berkshire Brewing Company
12 Railroad St., South Deerfield
413-665-6600
berkshirebrewingcompany.com

Founded in the early 1990s, this is one of New England's pioneering breweries, but it still has the craft-beer know-how and quality beer to keep up with the "kids" in the industry. A personal favorite of mine is the Raspberry Barleywine-Style Ale, made with half a pound per gallon of fresh raspberries from a local farm, only a few miles from the brewery. While this barley wine–style beer is sweet, it's also delicious, and is a must-buy each February when it's released.

Night Shift Brewing
87 Santilli Highway, Everett
617-294-4233
nightshiftbrewing.com

This serious, small, and experimental brewery has inspired many other serious, small, and experimental breweries in New England and beyond. While the vibe at the brewery itself is great, the beer is even better. The brewery was founded by three home-brewing friends who decided they didn't want to make beer that tasted just like many of the other beers being produced today. As a result, they are dedicated to creating unusual and memorable beers that also happen to be delicious. This is the little brewery that other little breweries want to be, and a brewery that beer lovers certainly want to visit.

Treehouse Brewing Company
162 East Hill Rd, Monson
413-523-2367
treehousebrew.com

Launched from a humble garage space, this brewery became a destination and holy beer-grimage for New England brew lovers who would lineup during the brewery's limited hours for growler fills. The brewery has announced plans to move from that humble space in Monson to Charlton in late 2017. With the move, it's clear the brewery has big plans and lots of great beer in store. "The intent of the new brewery is to make our beer better than ever, vastly expand our range of offerings, make our core offerings more readily available, and create a central gathering place of kinship and camaraderie for beer enthusiasts," according to an early 2016 blog post on the brewery's website.

Trillium Brewing Company
369 Congress St., Boston
617-453-8745
trilliumbrewing.com

In the heart of Boston this artisan farmhouse brewery creates incredible beer with local, native ingredients. The brewery owners strive to create the type of beers that "might have been made today, if a centuries-old beer culture had naturally evolved in New England." The sense of tradition is balanced with modern-day expertise, and the result is excellent beer. Trillium Brewing Company is fun to visit, and if you stop in, you'll quickly learn why this brewery has been making waves in the Boston craft-beverage scene.

Maine & New Hampshire

Majestic mountains and rocky coastlines provide a stunning backdrop for independent-minded brewers, distillers, and roasters.

Introduction

I couldn't keep up. There were just too many places.

Prior to my four-day tour of Portland, Maine, and Portsmouth, New Hampshire, and surrounding areas, I made a list of all the breweries, distilleries, and coffee shops in the region that I wanted to visit. The list looked good on paper. I'd be visiting three to four drinking establishments a day and one to two coffee shops. With a little discipline and a strict emphasis on sampling, getting to all the places on my list would be doable, and would not cause permanent medical damage.

What I didn't count on was the vibrancy of the craft-beverage scene in the two states. I kept hearing about new "must-try" locations while talking with people in taprooms and coffeehouses, and despite my promise before the trip to be "disciplined," I couldn't help but want to try the "new brewery down the road" or the distillery next door I hadn't previously heard about. I quickly realized that four days was not enough time to get a sense of the craft culture of the area, and more trips to both states would be in order.

As I headed south back toward my home in Connecticut, I couldn't help but think of two prominent figures from the region's past—one a pioneer of beer, and the other, quite the opposite.

Neal S. Dow is probably rolling over in his grave, but Frank Jones might just be smiling.

Both men were prominent politicians of the 1800s on opposite ends of the alcohol debate, and with spheres of influence in two major cities in neighboring states. Dow was mayor of Portland, Maine, in the 1850s and was an early zealot of Prohibition; as mentioned in this book's introduction, he successfully pushed for the passage of the Maine Law, which outlawed the sale of alcohol in 1851.

Jones was mayor of Portsmouth in the late 1860s, and a member of the US House of Representatives in the 1870s. His political career was funded by beer. Jones was the owner of the Frank Jones Brewing Company, which by 1882 was the largest producer of ale in the country. The company was so popular that a few years later it opened a satellite location in Boston. The Frank Jones Brewing Company survived Prohibition, but could not withstand the consolidation of the brewing industry following World War II, and was shuttered in 1950.

Today the legacies of both men live on in different ways, as Maine and New Hampshire have become regional craft powerhouses.

In Maine, beer, whiskey, gin, vodka, and alcoholic concoctions of almost every kind are being produced at a dizzying rate. In terms of breweries, Maine is one of the most saturated per capita states in the nation. Portland is a wonderland of brewing and distilling culture, with some sort of craft production site to be found at every corner—well, almost every corner. It all combines to make Portland, and Maine as a whole, one of the meccas of the craft world.

And that enthusiasm is spilling over the border. In New Hampshire a new generation of breweries and distillers are rediscovering the craft of their ancestors and the spirit of Frank Jones. Much of the industry is centered in and around Portsmouth, a historic port city that is one of the oldest in the country.

In the 1990s the craft movement in both Maine and New Hampshire was heavily influenced by the brewing traditions of England, Scotland, and Ireland. The brews produced were excellent, but not as experimental as what brewers on the West Coast were concocting. That has changed. In Portland, Allagash Brewing Company is dedicated to creating Belgian-style beer and bringing the Belgian brewing tradition of experimentation to the New World. In Portsmouth, Earth Eagle Brewings specializes in creating a medieval beer-like beverage called gruit that is made with a variety of herbs instead of hops. That skill and spirit of experimentation has carried over to the distilling world. Portland's Maine Craft Distilling makes a gin with carrots, while across town New England Distilling has painstakingly re-created the spirit production of yesteryear with inspiring results.

With all of these alcohol producers, the only saving grace for Dow is that at least there are plenty of nonalcoholic alternatives. In Portland there's so many great coffee shops that I began to wonder if the nation's most skilled baristas were confusing the Maine city with the other Portland in Oregon, and New Hampshire is home to one of my all-time favorite coffeehouses, the incomparable Caffe Kilim.

Beyond the beverages, the history and culture of the region, along with its natural and human-made beauty, is unmatched. Take in water views and summer concerts at Prescott Park in Portsmouth, enjoy the fresh local food in Portland, which has earned the city the designation of being one of the top foodie spots in the Northeast, and experience the culture of the sea in the Rockland and Rockport areas of Maine. Just remember: It may take a couple of trips to experience it all.

Portland, Part 1

The Trip

Like Dante says, "Midway upon the journey of our life I found myself within a forest dark, for the straightforward pathway had been lost." Then I spent a weekend in Portland, and things got better. This bustling Maine city is a hub of New England craft beverages overflowing with legitimate breweries, distilleries, and craft coffeehouses. Portland is one of the few places on the globe where you can go brewery-, distillery-, and craft coffeehouse–hopping, all on foot. During one epic day in the city, I visited six breweries, two distilleries, and three coffeehouses. (Don't worry; I had a designated driver, and made sure to pace myself.) The drinking scene here can't be summed up in one chapter, so I've devoted two to Portland.

In this first part, we take a closer look at **Rising Tide Brewing Company, Maine Craft Distilling,** and **Coffee By Design.** All three are located together—the brewery and distillery are literally next door to each other, and are across a quiet side street from the coffeehouse and roastery. Stopping by this cluster of craft-beverage perfection is the perfect way to experience the true spirit of this book all in one place. And while Portland makes for an excellent day trip, if you really want to dive into the craft-beverage scene of this city, I'd recommend making a weekend of it.

Highlights

The Beer
Rising Tide Brewing Company
No tour needed to get a peek.

The Booze
Maine Craft Distilling
Farm-to-flask distiller that locavores will love.

The Brew
Coffee By Design
Specialty coffee without the attitude, plus you can get a glimpse into the on-site roastery.

Maine Craft Distilling

THE BEER: Rising Tide Brewing Company
103 Fox St., Portland
207-307-2337
risingtidebrewing.com

When Nathan and Heather Sanborn had a son, they decided Heather, who had a law and teaching degree, would work while Nathan would be a stay-at-home dad. Yet Nathan's hobby, making beer, would prove to be more lucrative and rewarding than his wife's law career. Fascinated by the science and art of brewing, he became an accomplished home brewer. Once their son was old enough to be in school full-time, the Sanborns opened **Rising Tide Brewing Company.** It started as a nanobrewery (very small microbrewery), but quickly expanded. By 2015 the company's beer was being distributed across Maine as well as in Vermont, New Hampshire, and Massachusetts.

The brewery is next door to **Maine Craft Distilling.** In front of the entrance is a beer garden with the game cornhole setup. There are also food trucks on-site on weekends.

Tours are offered, but since the tasting room is in one corner of the brewery, you don't have to take a tour to get a peek at the brewing space. This is a family-run brewery, and Heather says that she and her husband view the staff as part of that extended family. The warmth and passion Nathan and Heather have for what they do shows in both the beer—which includes a year-round IPA and pale ale as well as more-experimental seasonal offerings—and the friendly way it is presented at the brewery.

"In our tasting room you can usually sample all of our core year-round brands, as well as some very limited beers that aren't available outside of Maine, and often even pilot brews that are not available outside the brewery," Heather says. "We'd recommend having a flight of samples when you visit so that you can try whatever is available that day."

Heather admits that running a brewery isn't the easiest of jobs. There are "lots of long hours, lots of evening marketing events followed by early-morning brew days," she says, but she's not pining away for her law career. "It's the best job in the world. We wouldn't trade it for anything. It's incredibly gratifying to be out at a bar and overhear someone commenting about how much they enjoy our beer. That makes the long days worth it."

On Tap

Seize the Daymark

Daymark American *Pale Ale* is a clean and crisp sessionable pale ale with a 5.5 ABV and a bright floral taste. Flavorful but not intensely hoppy or bitter, it is the perfect beer for the craft-beer newbie.

ABV: 5.5% IBUs: 42

Call me Ishmael

Ishmael American Copper is an American interpretation of the *altbiers*, a historic style of beer from Düsseldorf, Germany. This altbier is brewed with continental Munich malt, American-grown hops, and clean-fermenting ale yeast. The result is a slightly sweet and malty beer balanced by a firm bitterness. Availability: Year-round

ABV: 4.9% IBUs: 35

Word to the Weizen

Named for the little bear constellation, the *Ursa Minor* is a Weizen stout and the brewery's winter-wheat offering. Made with malted wheat and roasted malts, this beer tastes of dark fruit and roasted barley, and is the perfect companion for a cold winter's evening.

ABV: 6.7% IBUs: 30

Rising Tide Brewing Company
Photo by Foreside Photography

THE BOOZE: Maine Craft Distilling
101 Fox St., Portland
207-798-2528
mainecraftdistilling.com

Most distilleries are not as user-friendly as breweries. In general they're housed in nondescript industrial or corporate spaces, often without tasting rooms or with small tasting areas that are more of an afterthought than part of the place's original design. Thoroughly dedicated to function over form, they're the kind of places you visit if you're a huge fan of the product, not because it's a trendy new location you want to try. **Maine Craft Distilling** is an exception to that rule.

Located next door to Rising Tide, this distillery has a space worth seeing, whether you enjoy spirits or not. Loft-like and full of wood, the tasting room features two bars (both with seats) that overlook a cavernous and expertly laid-out distilling space. The tours are informal, which are my favorite. Try a few samples and then wander over and admire the distilling equipment. At Maine Craft Distilling, all spirits are made with locally grown ingredients, and great care is taken to make the distillation process as local and authentic to traditional techniques as possible.

It's no coincidence that Maine Craft Distilling has the feel of a brewery; after all, that was what founder Luke Davidson originally wanted to open. He realized, however, that "there are a lot of breweries already doing a great job," says Emily Davidson, Luke's sister, who in addition to her regular day job often can be found helping out at the distillery on weekends.

The idea for a Portland craft distillery that would complement the city's bustling brewing scene came to Luke one day while he was building a post-and-beam barn and musing about long-held dreams. He envisioned his distillery as a true "farm-to-flask" facility where no shortcuts would be taken in the production of spirits. Luke's vision attracted business partner Fred Farber, and in 2013 the dream of opening a craft distillery became a reality.

The distillery remains true to its founding ethos—mashing its own grain, using local agricultural products, and even working with a cooper to build the barrels used for aging spirits. The result is a product that is as inspiring as the city and space in which it was made.

Signature Booze

Carrot power

What's up, doc? The oh-so-very-unusual *Chesuncook Botanical Spirit* uses carrots—yes, carrots—as its base. Don't worry, it doesn't taste like the carrot juice you tried once after vowing that *this* was the year you were finally going to eat healthy. Instead it has a distinct (but not overpowering) carrot flavor that is balanced by juniper, mint, and coriander. I'm not going to lie and say I'm fully sold, but it's one of the more-distinctive New England spirits I've tried.

Strength: 90 proof

Kind of blue

Like any good moonshine, *Blueshine blueberry moonshine* will make your insides burn, and you'll feel it not just in your mouth but all the way down to your chest. This moonshine has a Maine twist: wild blueberries from the from Vacationland that cut the burn of the moonshine with blueberry sweetness.

Strength: 90 proof

Rationing rum

As recently as the 1970s, the British Navy provided daily rum rations to its crews. *Ration Expedition-Style Rum* is inspired by that practice. Distilled from molasses and aged for three months in heavily charred new oak barrels, it has an earthy color and flavor with notes of vanilla and oak. I'd gladly take a daily ration.

Strength: 90 proof

Maine
Craft Distilling

THE BREWS: Coffee By Design
1 Diamond St., Portland
207-879-2233
coffeebydesign.com

When Mary Allen Lindemann and her partner Alan Spear opened their first **Coffee By Design** coffee shop in 1994, there was a lot going against the new business. To begin with, downtown Portland had a vacancy rate of 40 percent. Then there was the fact that their original shop was on Congress Street, in what is now known as the Arts District but was then infamously known as the "porno district," because of the many adult theaters and adult stores in the neighborhood. Still, Lindemann and Spear saw beyond the vacant storefronts and smut-house cinemas to a historic area brimming with personality and ripe with opportunity.

"It was a location in a neighborhood where we knew people who lived and worked there," Lindemann recalls. "It was a really exciting time for us, being around other entrepreneurs and selling coffee."

On their first day open, they projected they would attract 25 customers, instead 250 came through the doors, and the people have been clamoring for Coffee By Design products ever since. That original storefront is still there at 620 Congress Street, but the business has wildly expanded. It has grown from a humble coffeehouse with a part-time barista to a Portland coffee-making powerhouse that has multiple locations with more than fifty full-time employees, distributing coffee far and wide from its micro-roastery. This roastery is of particular interest to liquid vacationers, in part because it's across a quiet side street and within easy walking distance from Maine Craft Distilling and Rising Tide, and also because it has a comfortable coffeehouse that allows guests to peek through large windows to see the roastery in action.

Lindemann has trademarked the phrase "specialty coffee without the attitude." Guests here can enjoy a wonderful tour of the high-end, specialty coffee-making world without having to feel left out if they're not familiar with the intricacies of the terminology. The Diamond Street coffee shop offers all your standard espresso-bar specialties. It's also a place where the staff is dedicated to coming up with new drinks and coffee flavors—from a pumpkin puree used to infuse lattes in the fall to cold-brewed coffee experimentations, including an El Salvador iced coffee split with ginger beer.

Although formal tours of the roastery aren't offered, informal ones are, and employees are happy to answer questions and explain the process. "We love to show people the space," Lindemann says. The building is 44,000 square feet and has room to accommodate four times the roastery's current capacity. The scale of the facility also allows the company to produce coffee more efficiently and in a more environmentally-friendly way, which helps keep coffee costs down.

Despite the company's growth, Lindemann says they have not lost their small-roastery feel. Each wholesale and retail order is roasted 100 percent to order, and Lindemann and Spear maintain the commitment to the quality on which the company was founded in that troubled Portland neighborhood all those years ago. "We believe everybody deserves to have a great cup of coffee," Lindemann says.

Signature Brews

Ice-ing

Lindemann explains that her staff has been experimenting with *iced coffee* in recent years. The Diamond Street roastery offers two rotating cold-brewed, iced-coffee options. These beans are picked for the flavor they add to cold-brewed coffee. A variety of outside-the-box, experimental iced drinks also are offered, from an iced coffee / ginger beer mix to Coffee By Design's version of an Arnold Palmer—cold-brewed coffee mixed with lemonade.

The dark side

The best-selling roaster product is *Alanzo's Double Dark* coffee. This robust blend is made from beans from Central and South America and is darker than midnight. But it's not dark like the Starbucks variety, with its charred, burnt taste; instead, you taste the nuances of the coffee's rich and smoky character.

Coffee By Design

Beyond the Beverages

Where to Eat

Portland is a food town. You can't throw a rock downtown without hitting a restaurant, and more are opening every day. If high-end cuisine interests you at all, stop by **Five Fifty-Five** (555 Congress St., Portland; 207-761-0555; fivefifty-five. com). Just about all you need to know about this Portland foodie favorite is that it offers a dish called "truffled lobster mac and cheese" featuring butter-poached Maine lobster, an artisanal cheese blend, white truffle oil, and black truffles. If that's not enough, the upscale restaurant also has special events like Oyster Thursdays, and features house-aged bourbon and spirit releases.

If that sounds too pricey, you can break bread with the locals at **Scratch Baking Co.** (416 Preble St., South Portland; 207-799-0668; scratchbakingco. com), where handmade bagels, English muffins, baguettes, and a variety of fresh-made breads and other savory baked sweets attract crowds. Get here early (like, before-nine-a.m. early) to ensure you get a bagel before supplies run out.

No visit to Maine would be complete without donuts. For great homemade, local donuts, try the **Holy Donut** (7 Exchange St., Portland, 207-775-7776; or 194 Park Ave., Portland, 207-874-7774; theholydonut.com).

And if you want a memorable lunch stop, complete with the best fries in town, **Duckfat** is the place to land (43 Middle St., Portland; 207-774-8080; duckfat.com).

If none of these appeal, just walk a block and you'll find a great place to eat.

Tapped Out / Where to Stay

It really takes more than a day to fully experience Portland's craft-beverage scene, so staying at least one night in the city is advised. Local options include the **Residence Inn Marriott** (145 Fore St., Portland; 207-761-1660; residenceinndowntownportland.com) and **Portland Harbor Hotel** (468 Fore St., Portland; 207-775-9090; portlandharborhotel.com). If you want a boutique experience, a swanky new place called **The Press Hotel** recently opened in the building which used to house the *Portland Press Herald* newspaper offices (119 Exchange St., Portland; 207-808-8800; thepresshotel.com).

Solid Side Trips

If you've tried all the featured beverage spots in this chapter and are still thirsting for more, first make arrangements to donate your liver to science, and then spend more time in the Fox Street area, in what locals informally call the "beverage district." Less than a quarter of a mile away from Rising Tide, Maine Craft, and Coffee By Design is another brewery and coffeehouse combo situated next to each other: **Bunker Brewery** (122 Anderson St., Portland; 207-450-5014; bunkerbrewingco.com) and **Tandem Coffee Roasters** (two locations: 122 Anderson St. and 742 Congress St., Portland; 207-899-0235; tandemcoffee.com).

Urban Farm Fermentory is a hop, skip, and a jump away, and features home-brewed kombucha and hard cider (200 Anderson St., Portland; 207-773-8331; urbanfarmfermentory.com). A half-mile away from them is **Maine Mead Works** (51 Washington Ave., Portland; 207-773-6323; mainemeadworks.com). Just pace yourself and remember the old adage of a wise craft drinker (aka, this author): "He or she who attempts to taste all in too short a period of time tastes nothing."

When you've finally tired of "swimming" the city's craft-beverage waters, try some actual swimming at one of the area beaches. In Portland guests can swim at the public **East End Beach** (Eastern Promenade, Portland). Neighboring South Portland is home to **Willard Beach** (southportland.org). It is a small sand-and-pebble beach where guests can swim or walk along the Spring Point Shoreway trail to the Spring Point Ledge Lighthouse, which has been in operation since 1897 at the entrance to Portland Harbor. If you have a yen to ride the high seas, take a ferry ride from the Casco Bay Lines ferry terminal (cascobaylines.com), or schedule a trip on the always-popular Downeast Duckboat Tour (downeastducktours.com).

Fresh Air

The problem with attempting to "walk it off" in Portland is that as you stroll the area around one brewery or bar, you inevitably stumble into another one, and without a lot of discipline your blood-alcohol level remains constant . . . or keeps rising. So you want to keep contact information handy for local cab companies, such as **ASAP Taxi** (207-791-2727; asaptaxi. net). Uber is also available in Portland.

That being said, there are some great walking destinations in the area, including **Peaks Island,** the largest of the islands surrounding Portland. Exploring it on foot is a great way to see some of the historic lighthouses (which Portland is known for) and to take in the sights and sounds of the surf. Or if you prefer to go downtown, a good resource for would-be walkers is the **Portland Trails** website (trails.org), which has information on more than 30 local walks.

Highlights

The Beer
Allagash Brewing Co.
A legend in the industry for their Belgian-style brews.

The Booze
New England Distilling
Uses a custom-designed, handmade copper pot still that is heated with direct fire, not steam.

The Brew
Speckled Ax
Roasts coffee by wood for a great flavor.

New England Distilling

Portland, Part 2

The Trip

For the second part of my trip to Portland, I visited Portland brewing giant **Allagash Brewing Company.** This Belgian-style brewing pioneer is across the street from three small breweries that also are worth checking out, and around the corner from **New England Distilling,** which is operated by Allagash's original head brewer, Ned Wight, who has opened his own distillery inspired by his family's distillation legacy and traditional techniques. From there we headed to downtown Portland to stop in at the no-nonsense coffeehouse, the **Speckled Ax,** where coffee perfection is strived for and, I'd argue, achieved.

 THE BEER:
Allagash Brewing Company
50 Industrial Way, Portland
207-878-5385
allagash.com

For hundreds of years, monks in Belgium and other parts of Europe have been making a different kind of holy water—beer. Monastery brewhouses, where monks brew, sell, and of course drink beer, have existed since the Middle Ages. The tradition of monastic brewing helped to fuel the innovative, distinct, and often experimental style of Belgian beer. Although extremely devout holy men developed it, Belgian beer is, surprisingly, all about breaking the rules.

"Belgian-style brewing is very much about creativity and unique ingredients, or really, a lack of style," explains Jason Perkins, brewmaster at **Allagash Brewing Company.** "With German beer, which I absolutely love, it's a very strict brewing tradition. The Belgians almost take the opposite approach."

Perkins says much of this style's flavor is derived from the yeast. "Just like you could describe a great IPA as a hop-forward beer, in a lot of cases a Belgian-style beer is more of a yeast-forward beer."

Perkins's boss, Rob Tod, founded Allagash in 1995 and brought Belgian-style "yeast-forward beer" to the masses of Maine and elsewhere. Tod was inspired by Pierre Celis, a Belgian milkman-turned-brewer who revived *witbier*, then an endangered species of beer, in Belgium at the Hoegaarden Brewery, and then in Texas at the now-defunct Celis Brewery. When Tod was thinking about opening his brewery, the craft-beer revolution in Portland was just beginning to get going. **Shipyard Brewing Company** had opened in the city the previous year, and many more breweries were on the way. Breweries in Maine and most of New England, however, were more dedicated to creating hearty English- and Scottish-style IPAs and ales. "There was nobody in New England doing anything remotely like Belgian-style beers at the time," Perkins says.

The brewery's flagship beer is **Allagash White Ale,** a classic *witbier* that has won multiple World Beer Cup gold medals and remains the brewery's best-selling product. Initially, it wasn't always very well-received. Because specific yeasts are left within the beer, it has a cloudy appearance, almost like there's sediment in the bottle. At first, this turned people off. Perkins started at the brewery

Trappist Ales

Bar Trivia

The majority of beer brewed at monasteries in Belgium and is made by the Trappist order, a devout and traditionally cloistered group of Catholic monks. The order originated in the Cistercian monastery of La Trappe, France, when a reform movement started in 1664 in reaction to the relaxation of practices in many Cistercian monasteries. The Trappists, or Order of the Strict Observance, placed a renewed emphasis on living simply and supporting themselves and their monasteries by "the work of their hands."

As a result, many Trappist monasteries produced goods such as bread, cheese, or (you guessed it) beer. During the French Revolution and then during Napoleon's rule, many monks from the order fled France and settled in various parts of Europe. As of this book's writing, there were ten officially recognized Trappist breweries in the world, including six in Belgium (among them Chimay and Orval) and one in the United States (**Spencer Brewery,** makers of **Spencer Trappist Ale,** which is brewed by the monks of St. Joseph's Abbey in Spencer, Massachusetts).

in 1999, and even then he recalls, "You'd go to events and brew fests and visit accounts and get a lot of feedback from people saying, 'This beer is cloudy. Why does this beer look like this? Why does this beer smell like this?' We even used to hear 'Your beer is infected.' It was always our battle to educate the consumers on what it was and the history behind the beer style and its intricacies," he says.

It's a battle Perkins and company have won. Over the years Allagash has grown into one of the biggest breweries in New England, and one of the fifty most successful craft breweries in the country. Guests who make the Belgian-style beer pilgrimage to Allagash find themselves in a wooded corporate park area outside downtown Portland. Inside the brewery, good news awaits: Each guest can enjoy a free flight of the four beers available on tap that day—great for the budget-conscious liquid vacationer. The taproom is spacious, with easy access to a gift shop that offers lots of Allagash bling. In the warmer months there's a nice outdoor beer garden.

The tours last about forty-five minutes and are conducted by knowledgeable brewery staff. During the tour guests can see the bottling and kegging lines as well as the barrel-aging room. They're also taken through a guided tasting. Though the samples at Allagash are free, each guest is limited to one flight of samples per day. But after tearing through those samples, you can leave your car parked at Allagash and walk across the street to a corporate building that is home to three—yes, three—craft breweries, at 1 Industrial Way: **Bissell Brothers** (207-808-8258; bissellbrothers.com), **Foundation Brewing Company** (207-370-8187; foundationbrew.com), and **Austin Street Brewery** (207-200-1994; austinstreetbrewery.com). All three are small, experimental, and intriguing breweries with potential to grow. It was in the exact same building that **Rising Tide** and **Maine Beer Company** both got their start before moving to bigger

Bar Trivia

Keeping it Coolship

A coolship is a large shallow pan used to cool wort overnight using outside air temperature. During the cooling process, naturally occurring yeast from the air inoculates the wort, the liquid extracted during the mashing process. In the morning, the cooled wort is transferred into barrels where the fermentation process begins, often resulting in wild fermented ales. Anchor Brewing Company in San Francisco has long used a modern form of open fermentation, but Allagash is believed to be the first US brewery to employ the traditional style of open fermentation. Many have since followed in its oh-so-very-*cool* footsteps.

Allagash Brewing Company

facilities. Not far from this brewery grouping is the **D. L. Geary Brewing Company** (38 Evergreen Dr., Portland; 207-878-2337; gearybrewing.com).

Perkins is genuinely proud to be a part of this robust brewing and craft-beverage community, and like its little siblings in the brewing world, Allagash continues to keep the spirit of craft-brewing experimentation alive and well. The brewery has seven year-round beers, as well as multiple specialty and limited-release beers, including barrel-aged and sour beers fermented with wild yeast. And in keeping with the Belgian brewing traditions of old, Allagash continues to innovate while avoiding making too many rules for themselves in the brewing process. "We don't like to put ourselves in any boxes here," Perkins says.

On Tap

White out
Allagash White is the one that started it all for Allagash. Light-bodied, delicious, and refreshing, it is brewed with wheat and spiced with coriander and Curacao orange peel. This beer has a compelling balance of spice and fruit flavors that lives up to its reputation.
ABV: 5% IBUs: 20

Tripel threat
Strong and golden **Allagash Tripel Ale** has intense fruit flavors with herbal notes and hints of banana and honey—a wonderful example of this delicious beer. However, like many tripels, it's deceptively high in alcohol, and it's easy to drink more of it than you realize, so be careful and remember to sip slowly.
ABV: 9% IBUs: 35

In the red
Allagash Coolship Red is part of the brewery's coolship series, a group of beers made using naturally occurring wild yeast. Aged for six months in oak wine barrels that are each filled with one hundred pounds of fresh Maine raspberries, this bright red beer has a tart and dry flavor that makes it a favorite of wine and beer drinkers alike.
ABV: 5.7% IBUs: 22

THE BOOZE: New England Distilling
26 Evergreen Drive, Unit B, Portland
207-878-9759
newenglanddistilling.com

Ned Wight was the head brewer at Allagash from 1996 to 2002. It was a dream come true for him to help pioneer Belgian-style brewing in the United States and to be part of one of the most influential craft breweries around. Yet, as Wight is fond of telling people, it was only the second-best job he ever had.

The "best job" distinction belongs to his current position as distiller and owner of **New England Distilling** (which he abbreviates as "NED"). This distillery is around the corner from Allagash in a quiet corporate building, set in a wooded area outside downtown Portland. While Allagash offers guests a chance to experience New World Belgian-style beer, Wight's distillery offers a journey back in time to the glory days of America's distilling past. It's a journey filled with heart, insight, and, yes, some excellent samples of distilled products.

With dark curly hair and a friendly appearance, Wight is often on hand when the distillery is open to the public for tastings and tours. A veteran of the world of craft brewing and distilling, Wight says craft distilling was a logical progression from the craft-beer movement, but he and his fellow distillers still have some catching up to do. "[Craft distilling now] feels like the craft-beer movement in the early '90s," he says.

Opening a distillery wasn't just a way for Wight to take part in a burgeoning American craft movement; it was also a chance to reignite the torch of a family legacy. In the 1850s, Wight's great-great-great-grandfather, John Jacob Wight, opened a distillery north of Baltimore in the Hunt Valley of Maryland. Family members continued that business for generations, even surviving a forced closure during Prohibition. But in 1958, due to changing tastes, the last family distillery closed its doors. More than half a century later, Wight has revived the family legacy in Maine. Although his eyes are on the future, his feet are rooted firmly in the past.

"I feel very strongly that technology has its place, and so, too, does history," he writes on his website. "Distilling is one of those crafts that offer a unique meeting ground between history and technology, art and science. When I am creating something, I want to get close to it, get my hands on it and get involved; I'd rather turn a valve than press a button. I believe that every valve turn, every flame adjustment, and every bucket poured add to the final product like a brush stroke. At New England Distilling we blend history and technology—with a little more history, maybe."

Wight's distillery uses a custom-designed, handmade copper pot still that is heated with direct fire, rather than steam. He explains that the direct fire method causes more caramelizing reactions in the pot, leading to a more complex, robust spirit. Wight makes three spirits: a rum, a rye whiskey, and a gin. Each is full of character and flavor, and does his family's rich distilling legacy proud. And Wight hasn't forgotten his brewing background, either. He maintains a close relationship with Allagash, which gives him the bourbon barrels in which he ages his rum. After using these barrels, Wight returns some of them to Allagash for the specialty release of a rum-barrel-aged brown sour beer named "Neddles," in his honor. Wight says his brewing expertise helps him to create his distilled products, because "you don't really make flavor in a still. You make flavors during fermentation."

Signature Booze

Dry your eyes
Ingenium Dry Gin is named for the word *ingenium,* defined as the engine of natural creativity that comes from observation and imagination. Once your taste buds "observe" this traditional-style gin, your imagination will run wild. The distillery's direct-fired pot still allows this gin to retain the flavors of the grain, giving it a mouthfeel that is reminiscent of whiskey. This combines with citrus and herb flavors, making this spirit a must-try gin.
Strength: 94 proof

The catcher and rye whiskey
New England Distillery's *Gunpowder Rye Whiskey* draws its inspiration from Wight's family distilling tradition. It is brewed from local grains and distilled in small batches. The result is a spicy Maryland-style rye with toasted-malt flavor and a long finish with vanilla and chocolate notes.
Strength: 87 proof

Ring them bells
Eight Bells Rum is a barrel-matured gold rum. Distilled from Caribbean-sourced molasses in the distillery's pot still and then aged for a year in bourbon whiskey barrels, it has a flavor of toasted spice and vanilla and a long, smooth finish with hints of caramel, oak, and figs modeled after early New England rums. Name inspired by Maine artist, Winslow Homer, whose studio is located in Scarborough, Maine.
Strength: 90 proof

THE BREWS: Speckled Ax
567 Congress St., Portland
207-660-3333
speckledax.com

There are serious coffee shops, and then there's the **Speckled Ax.** At this new-wave establishment, which opened in 2012, the coffee used is not only roasted by the cafe's sister company, **Matt's Coffee,** it's organic *and* wood-roasted, as in roasted with a fire fueled by wood.

The cafe takes its name from a passage in Ben Franklin's autobiography about shooting for moral perfection, and perfection in general, but inevitably falling short, resulting in a proverbial "speckled axe" rather than an untarnished gleaming blade. The Speckled Ax is all about obtaining coffee-making perfection.

When I stopped in for an incognito visit (whenever possible, I didn't announce myself in advance), I happened to meet owner Matt Bolinder. He's tall, with dark hair and a serious demeanor.

"For centuries, coffee beans were roasted over a wood fire, but most modern roasting equipment is built for use with natural gas, propane, or electricity," he writes. "With such fuels, there's no cutting, splitting, drying, or lugging, and temperatures can be controlled with the touch of a button or turn of a knob. Progress has its advantages, but if you're like us, you can appreciate the old-fashioned way of doing certain things as well. There's something inherently pleasing in the snap of a stick of rock maple and the dance of an open flame. Using wood to roast a historically ceremonial and eminently sociable comfort food feels right—especially here in New England."

But there's more: Roasting the coffee by wood also adds to the aroma and taste of the finished product.

"While the beans are roasted through contact with the drum wall, the primary exchange of heat is not conduction, but convection—that is, hot air from the wood fire passing over and through the bean mass," Bolinder writes. "Our wood-fire roasting process results in an additional layer of nuanced aromatics and an exceptionally smooth brew."

I immediately understood that last part when I tried the coffee at Speckled Ax. It's the kind that grabs hold of your taste buds and cries "Remember me"—and you will. This coffee is intense, bold, and full of flavor. Pour-overs are prepared with reverence and skill, the cappuccino comes with a glass of sparkling water, and if you smell your coffee and then sip it slowly, letting each separate flavor sink into your mouth, no one will look at you funny. This might be too intense for the casual coffee drinker, but if you're a hard-core coffee fan, this is an ax you'll want to grind. Although the coffee produced at Speckled Ax still may have its "speckles," I couldn't find them.

Signature Brews

Dog eat dog

The Bird Dog blend from Matt's Coffee, which is sold at Speckled Ax, will give you a pick-me-up even if it's a dog-day afternoon. This northern-Italian-style espresso has five different coffees and contrasts with the more common dark and often oily southern Italian-style espresso. Mellow and sweet, it can be drunk as a straight shot or enjoyed in an espresso or other drink.

Map of the world

Map 40 Mokha Java's description states "Mokha Java is commonly thought of as the oldest of blends, originating in the early eighteenth century." The Speckled Ax / Matt's Coffee version of this ancient blend combines lots of darkly roasted Ethiopian beans with darkly roasted organic Java, and then adds a fruity medium-roast natural Ethiopian as well as a smattering of lightly roasted Ethiopian coffee.

Serious foam

As I mentioned earlier, **cappuccino** is one of my favorite drinks of any kind, and my go-to at any coffee shop I visit. So over the last year and half I've drunk a *lot* of cappuccinos, both while researching this book and just in everyday life. The cappuccino at Speckled Ax really stands out above the masses. Served with sparkling water to cleanse the palate, this biting, bitter, and intensely flavorful cappuccino makes me want to, like the old song says, "throw my hands up and shout."

Highlights

The Beer
Oxbow Brewing Co.
Loud beer from a quiet place in the Maine woods.

The Booze
Sweetgrass Farm Winery & Distillery
Situated on a seventy-acre farm with breathtaking panoramic views.

The Brew
Rock City Café
Features rotating coffees and a charming bookstore in the back.

Sweetgrass Farm

Rockland and Rockport

The Trip
In search of craft-beverage perfection, I ventured north along the eastern coastline into the heart of Maine, where the sounds and signs of civilization grew sparser and the voice and power of the sea more apparent. Here the ghosts of pirates are said to lurk above the waves, and the sea air hits your lungs with an invigorating freshness not felt in more-crowded parts of the globe.

But the salted water of the sea was not what brought me here; I was drawn by a different kind of liquid. After setting up my base of operations in Rockport, I ventured further afield than usual. First, I visited **Oxbow Brewing Company,** a true American farmhouse brewery in Newcastle, about 45 minutes south of Rockport. Then I went to **Rock City Café,** a hip downtown artisan coffeehouse in Rockland, a town that neighbors Rockport; before heading about twenty minutes inland to **Sweetgrass Farm Winery & Distillery,** on the grounds of a beautiful farm in Union.

Rockport is about four hours north of Boston and two north of Portland, Maine. A trip here allows you to experience great beverages in beautiful, natural settings. If you detest city life, chart your course for winding country roads and quiet seaside towns where the harbor is filled with wooden ships and your glass is filled with craft-beverage perfection.

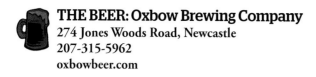

THE BEER: Oxbow Brewing Company
274 Jones Woods Road, Newcastle
207-315-5962
oxbowbeer.com

If you travel off the beaten path just a bit you'll be rewarded with liquid art from the **Oxbow Brewing Company.** Billed as making "loud beer from a quiet place," this brewery makes Belgian-style farmhouse ales at a facility located, fittingly, in a converted barn on the grounds of a Newcastle farm.

The brewery was founded in 2011 by Geoff Masland and Tim Adams. "Geoff and I were both passionate beer lovers and we'd both been in the industry for a while," recalls Adams, who also serves as director of brewing operations. "I was a home brewer, and we were really liking the beers that I was putting together by taking a unique approach to farmhouse brewing."

Masland and his wife own a beautiful Newcastle property with a barn on it that Masland and Adams thought would make a perfect brewery. Today that converted barn makes all the GPS toggling worth it by rewarding travelers with an outrageously good beer experience.

For a less rustic but still rewarding beer experience, stop by the **Oxbow Blending & Bottling** satellite tasting room at 49 Washington Avenue in Portland, behind **Coffee By Design** (see "Portland, Part 1" page 65). Both offer the chance to try fresh samples of the brewery's product, but the actual brewery gives more insight into the farmhouse philosophy that permeates the beer and the brand.

"Traditional farmhouse ale brewing is a unique way to make beer and a unique mind set and philosophical standpoint on making beer," Adams explains. "We like using local ingredients. We are, to a certain extent, reactive to our surroundings. If the local winery has a unique wine barrel, we'll snatch it up and make a beer around it."

These creative products include a variety of barrel-aged beers and sour beers fermented with wild yeast. These experimental offerings are released through Oxbow's Freestyle Series, beers that generally are only brewed once and can be hard to find outside the brewery or the Portland tasting room. There also is a collection of regular and recurring offerings from the brewery, including the **Farmhouse Pale Ale.**

The laid-back vibe at the brewery itself makes for an excellent trip. On the casual informal tours, guests can visit the grounds of the property, where some of the fruit for various beers are grown. A trip to this brewery is as light and refreshing as its flagship Farmhouse Pale Ale.

On Tap

The Oxbow incident

Part of the fun of visiting a brewery like Oxbow is trying some of the rotating beers and special releases—the brews that are difficult to find anywhere but at the brewery. Past beers brewed as part of Oxbow's Freestyle Series have included the **Smoked Chocolate Stout** and **Black Wheat Saison**, as well as a variety of IPAs and saisons. The regularly brewed beers here include the aforementioned **Farmhouse Pale Ale,** as well as **Space Cowboy Country Ale,** a dry *biere de garde* (a strong pale ale-style farmhouse ale) and Grizacca an American take on the classic but obscure farmhouse beer style known as *grisette* (another farmhouse ale that is lighter than a saison, a far more common style of farmhouse ale).

THE BOOZE: Sweetgrass Farm Winery & Distillery
347 Carroll Road, Union
207-785-3024
sweetgrasswinery.com

Forget the warehouse, industrial-style beverage destinations and enjoy a distilling oasis that has the beauty of an actual oasis at **Sweetgrass Farm Winery & Distillery.** This Maine craft distillery is situated on a seventy-acre farm with hiking trails, a picnic area, garden, and breathtaking panoramic views of the Medomak River valley.

Though Sweetgrass is a winery, don't be fooled by that title—the farm is not actually a vineyard. Instead of grapes, it is home to livestock, including sheep and chickens, and the wine is made from local fruit like apples, blueberries, and cranberries. Brandy and a variety of gins are also produced. The winery and distillery are open to the public from Mother's Day till New Year's Day, but the company also operates the **Portland Old Port Tasting Room & Shop** (324 Fore St., Portland; 207-761-8GIN) that is open all year. If you can time your visit right, a trip to the winery and distillery is more fun, and will give you a better feel for the business and the couple who started it.

Keith and Constance Bodine purchased the farm in 2005 to start their winery and distillery. Keith has an undergraduate degree in engineering and a master's degree in food science, and is a thirty-year veteran of the distilling and winemaking world.

"He worked at many wineries and distilleries and built both all over the world before we came home here to do it for ourselves," his wife says. "We were married here thirty years ago. My family's from Maine, and when Keith saw Maine, he loved it, and we knew we wanted to raise a family here."

Formal tours are not offered, but the tasting room overlooks the farm, and Keith and Constance often are on hand to answer questions while guests sample up to five drinks each. People usually go for a variety of drinks, Constance says, trying at least one wine, one liqueur, and then other types of spirits. All told, Sweetgrass is a wonderful experience for craft-beverage adventurers. It's the kind of farm you imagine visiting in Europe while sipping fine Old Country spirits. If the weather is nice, pack a picnic lunch before sampling some products in the tasting room, and then buy a bottle of something you enjoyed and sit back and take in the fresh Maine air.

Signature Booze

Rolling on the river

Back River Gin is a gin drinker's gin, and one of the most acclaimed spirits at the distillery. It is made in the London tradition, but with a healthy burst of Maine in the form of blueberries. The combination of botanicals and blueberries gives this gin a refreshing taste.
Strength: 86 Proof

Crow-ing on

The distillery's *Three Crow Rum* is made from top-grade cane molasses that is fermented and distilled during the cold Maine winter and then aged in bourbon barrels. The final product is an ultra-smooth rum with hints of caramel and butterscotch.
Strength: 80 Proof

An Apple Brandy a day

Local apples are blended and distilled into the company's *Apple Brandy.* Each bottle contains the essence of forty apples and is aged for thirty-six months, creating a beverage with fresh apple aromas and pecan and crème brûlée flavors.
Strength: 80 Proof

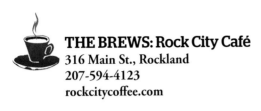

THE BREWS: Rock City Café
316 Main St., Rockland
207-594-4123
rockcitycoffee.com

In the early 1990s Susanne Ward and her husband, the late Patrick Reilley, realized the East Coast was still stuck in the coffee dark ages.

"We had lived in California and were really spoiled by the coffee out there," she says. Back in Maine, she recalls, people considered Green Mountain French Vanilla to be gourmet coffee. To shine some light into this coffee wilderness, in 1992 the couple opened **Second Read Books & Coffee,** a coffeehouse and bookstore combo in Rockland. Over the years the business grew and changed into **Rock City Café** and **Rock City Roasters.** Both the roastery and coffeehouse portions of the business are staples of the city, and are open to the public, giving liquid vacationers a chance to watch a micro coffee roaster in action while also visiting a hip cafe and coffeehouse.

Rock City Café, located at 316 Main Street, is a fun and eclectic coffee shop featuring a variety of specialty rotating coffees that also are available as pour-overs. It serves coffee cocktails and craft beer, has house-made pastries and a full small-plates menu, and features acoustic music several nights a week. It's the kind of place you wish you could go once a week and join with the regulars. The bookstore portion of the business was sold in 2011 to a coffeehouse employee and rebranded as **hello hello books,** so there still is ample opportunity for joint coffee drinking and book browsing.

Just a few blocks down at 215 Main Street, coffee connoisseurs can get a view of the roasting process at **Rock City Roasters.** The roastery has a coffee bar with a full line of coffee and pastries, and there's also room to sit back and relax. "They can watch the roasting and the action and we can talk to people about what they like and even do proprietary blends and special roasts for them," Ward says. "It's a fun place for the really geeky coffee people." She adds, "The café is really more of a social place, and the other one is more of a serious coffee place."

Both locations offer a rotating lineup of coffees that usually includes a dark roast, an organic roast, a single-origin coffee, a decaf, and maybe a flavored coffee. Liquid vacationers with a passion for coffee will want to visit both to experience their individual charms.

Signature Brews

Ice, Ice Baby
The excellent artisan coffee at Rock City Café and Rock City Roasters comes in a variety of forms. The ***iced coffee*** is the most popular item all year, even during the winter. We also recommend trying a single-origin coffee and a ***coffee cocktail,*** because it's not often you get a chance to enjoy a great cup of coffee infused with alcohol.

Single-Origin Coffee Explained

As you explore high-end coffee culture, you'll come across the term *single-origin coffee* on more than one occasion. Essentially, single-origin is coffee made with beans from a single region—ideally, a small region or even a single farm, and *not* a blend of beans from different regions. That seems straightforward enough, but sometimes the politics of coffee terminology can be more divisive and confusing than the health-care debate.

A single-origin coffee simply could mean the beans come from a single country, which may not tell you much about the climate or region where the coffee beans were harvested, especially if you're dealing with a country as large and geographically diverse as, say, Brazil. To combat some of this vagueness and add another level of specialty and flavor, some coffeehouses and roasters feature *estate coffee*—coffee grown at one estate or farm—and *micro-lot coffee*—coffee made from beans harvested from a single field on a farm. Usually this field is chosen because the beans in this area are particularly special in terms of flavor.

Bar Trivia

Beyond the Beverages

Where to Eat

If you want something different than the lunch-style, small-plates menu at Rock City Café, try **Shepherd's Pie**, a farm-to-table hot spot with an excellent beer list (18 Central St., Rockport; 207-236-8500; shepherdspierockport.com). For breakfast and lunch, try **Home Kitchen Cafe** (650 Main St., Rockland; 207-596-2449; homekitchencafe.com) a former *Yankee Magazine* Best Breakfast winner, it is full of local flavor and will more than satisfy your comfort food cravings.

Tapped Out / Where to Stay

Drop anchor for the night at **Strawberry Hill Seaside Inn** (886 Commercial St., Rockport; 207-594-5462; strawberryhillseasideinn.com), where you'll enjoy ocean views, a private patio or deck with each room, and access to a heated outdoor pool. You also can do far more than just hunker down for the night at **Samoset Resort on the Ocean** (220 Warrenton St., Rockport; 207-594-2511; samosetresort.com), a historic estate that was built in 1902 and is perched on 230 waterfront acres. In the summer you can lounge at the pool, hot tub, and poolside bar, and in the winter guests can enjoy the Glacier Ice Bar, a bar carved from ice that is the centerpiece of an upscale outdoor lounge with fires and plenty of specialty cocktails to keep you warm.

Solid Side Trips

One of the things I love to do most in the Rockport-Camden area is book a short voyage on a schooner it's an unparalleled chance to explore the coastline. My favorite is the schooner *Heron* (docked at Rockport Marine Park, 111 Pascal Ave., Rockport; 207-236-8605; sailheron.com). Captained by Nigel Bower and Bonnie Schmidt, this beautiful wooden ship winters in the Caribbean and was featured in the Johnny Depp film, *The Rum Diary*.

If sailing for the day seems too much of a departure from the craft-beverage program, you can continue your explorations with a trip to **Marshall Wharf Brewing Company** and its sister bar, **Three Tides** (2 Pinchy Ln., Belfast; 207-338-1707; 3tides.com). The innovative and quirky brewery and bar have a true seaside-town, tugboat feel, and, as if that wasn't enough, they've even used seaweed as an ingredient in their beer. Word is that it's far better-tasting than it sounds.

Bonus Brewery

Maine Beer Company
Maine Beer Company
525 US Route 1, Freeport
207-221-5711
mainebeercompany.com

When David and Dan Kleban started their brewery in a building across the street from Allagash Brewing Company in Portland, Maine, their brewing system was so small that it seemed microscopic even when compared to other small breweries. This was 2009, and the concept of a nanobrewery was still alien to many people, so when the brothers opened their **Maine Beer Company** armed only with a one-barrel brewing system and a variety of hop-forward recipes they had developed as home brewers, many saw them as destined for failure.

Dan recalls people routinely telling them: "You can't start that way; that won't work." But the Kleban brothers were no dummies. Dan is a litigation lawyer by trade and his brother is a financial adviser. Before giving up their successful day jobs, they wanted to test the waters and see how people reacted to their beer. Opening on a small scale seemed the perfect way to do that.

It worked and the brewery's small-batch beer soon became the stuff of legends. In 2011, the *Boston Globe* wrote a story about how **Lunch IPA** had become one of the most sought-after beers in the country. Dan kept working as a lawyer at first, brewing on weekends and evenings as time allowed. As the brewery became more successful, he shifted to part-time work as a lawyer. Now he works full-time

Fresh Air

There is the opportunity for some casual strolling at **Oxbow Brewing Company** and some great hiking trails on the property of **Sweetgrass Farm Winery & Distillery**. Downtown Rockland and Camden are wonderful places to enjoy on foot. This area is not cab-friendly, so if you don't feel like "walking it off," bring a designated driver and go easy on the samples.

at the brewery, and Maine Beer Company has outgrown its nanobrewery roots.

The company currently operates a sleek, visitor-friendly, fifteen-barrel brewhouse north of Portland, in Freeport. Although no tours are offered, the large, comfortable taproom overlooks the brewery floor, allowing visitors to see all the action on brewing days. Guests can enjoy a variety of the brewery's regular offerings, or one of its "pilot beers," a rotating series of small-batch test beers made from experimental recipes. Dan says these beers give "people that actually come to the brewery the opportunity to try something that they really can't try anywhere else."

One of the first craft beers Dan fell in love with was Sierra Nevada Pale Ale, and that beer and beers like it provide inspiration for the brewery. The Kleban brothers wanted to produce hops-forward American ales in the style of those being produced on the West Coast, and wanted to deliver them to New England consumers quickly, which they believed would make a difference in the flavor.

"Hoppy beers in particular are very susceptible to degradation over time," Dan explains. "That punchy hops flavor and aroma are the first things that disappear from the beer as it grows old."

That's part of the reason the brewery is obsessed with age. Each beer is bottled with a date on it, and it's strongly recommended that you drink it before it's more than 90 days old. (Waiting longer won't make you sick or anything like that; it just won't taste quite as good.)

Despite the hop-forward nature of the brewery's beers, Maine Beer Company is not about producing tongue-rippers or overly bitter beers; instead, hops are used to provide the flavor and aroma.

"Our beers are very balanced, and they're all very clean; the yeast is really neutral in them, and it lets the hops shine in a natural way," Dan says. "We're not a brewery that does a lot of over-the-top styles; we really like to focus on the delicacy of the beer, the balance of the beer, and let that speak for itself."

Still, the brewery does have a little bit of a wild side that comes across in some of its barrel-aging programs, including a barrel-aged blend of two beers called the **Sour Funky Ale.**

Maine Beer has proved the naysayers wrong, and in the process helped to pioneer the concept of starting as a small nanobrewery, building a following, and then expanding into a bigger brewery. On the path to its success, the brewery has remained socially conscious; many of the beer names are inspired by ecological or animal-welfare causes, and 1 percent of gross sales are donated to environmental nonprofits. There's nothing like drinking a great beer for a great cause.

Maine Beer Company

On Tap

Lunch break

The *Lunch IPA* is what put Maine Beer Company on the map, and it's a beer that will put a visit to this brewery on your travel itinerary. Intense hop flavors and aromas of pine and tropical and citrus fruits dominate, balanced by a subtle malt sweetness.

ABV: 7%

Peep peep

Peeper, the brewery's original hoppy American ale, still gets the job done. It is dry, clean, and well-balanced, with a generous dose of American hops. It's a wonderful introduction to the brewery's beers.

ABV: 5.5%

Weez-er

Weez is a dark American IPA that has a blend of hoppy and roasty notes on the nose, followed by hoppy resins on the tongue. It finishes with a deep and distinctive roast.

ABV: 7.2%

Tributary Brewing   Photo by www.erikjensen.io

Atlantic Brewing

Another Round: Maine

Atlantic Brewing Company
15 Knox Road, Bar Harbor
207-288-2337
atlanticbrewing.com

This brewery provides quite the visitor experience, offering tours, tastings, and an outdoor eatery called **Mainely Meat Barbecue**. Pair barbecue favorites like a rack of ribs and pulled pork with beers such as **Bar Harbor Summer Ale,** a delicious hybrid of an English ale and a German lager. There is also house-made, nonalcoholic blueberry soda and root beer for the younger members of your entourage. The brewery and barbecue is open from Memorial Day weekend to mid-October, so plan accordingly.

Boothbay Craft Brewery
301 Adams Pond Road, Boothbay
207-633-3411, boothbaycraftbrewery.com

Located on the grounds of the Boothbay Resort, a small cottage resort in operation since 1955, this is a great destination brewery. Stay in one of the resort's cozy cottages and enjoy a freshly brewed ale while relaxing by the pool or playing bocce. Beers are made in part utilizing hops that are grown on the resort grounds and a nearby hopyard. This is one brewery that espouses a truly local philosophy.

Funky Bow Brewery & Beer Company

21 Ledgewood Lane, Lyman
207-423-9348
funkybowbeercompany.com

You have to love a brewery with slogans like "It's the yeast we could do" and beer names like **So Folkin' Hoppy IPA.** If that's not enough, every Friday this brewery fires up a wood oven and makes pizza with dough using spent grain from the brewery and local ingredients. This pizza is offered free to beer drinkers—yes, free pizza! On top of that, the beer is excellent and as the brewers say, "Nothing at Funky Bow is plain and/or normal; our beers will always challenge your taste buds in the best of ways."

Tributary Brewing Company

10 Shapleigh Road, Kittery
207-703-0093
tributarybrewingcompany.com

Across the water from Portsmouth, New Hampshire, Kittery is a beautiful up-and-coming Maine town that has been called Portsmouth's version of Brooklyn. When it comes to craft beverages, the small town lives up to that nickname. A bustling beverage scene is anchored by Tributary Brewing Company, a hometown brewery that makes a variety of IPAs and seasonal and specialty beers. The brewery frequently hosts live music and is fun to visit. If you stop by, also consider visiting the nearby **Blue Current Brewery** (65 US Route 1 Bypass, Kittery; 617-797-9876; bluecurrent.net), one of only a handful of sake producers in the United States.

Funky Bow Brewery

Portsmouth, Part 1

The Trip

Portsmouth, New Hampshire, is a beautiful coastal city that was settled in 1623 and lays claim to being the third-oldest city in the nation. It also has an excellent craft-beverage scene with a long-established craft-brewing presence, a thriving cafe culture, and an emerging craft-distilling presence. About an hour north of Boston and about an hour south of Portland, Maine, this tourist-friendly city makes for a wonderful day trip or weekend getaway. Because of the city and surrounding area's thriving craft-beer scene, I've devoted two chapters to Portsmouth.

In Part 1, I take a closer look at **Earth Eagle Brewings,** an innovative downtown brewery, and **Caffe Kilim,** a legendary coffeehouse with a Turkish flair. Then I venture outside the city for a trip to **Flag Hill,** a winery and distillery situated on a beautiful vineyard.

The Beer: Earth Eagle Brewings
165 High St., Portsmouth
603-817-2773
eartheaglebrewings.com

The brewers at **Earth Eagle Brewings,** a brewery and pub, are enthusiasts of a different kind of herb. For hundreds of years in medieval Europe, beer often was made without the addition of hops, using instead a variety of herbs. The obviously less-hoppy beverages these herbs produced were called gruits, pronounced "groot," like fruit with a "G." Over the centuries *gruit*, which comes from the old German word for "root," fell out of favor. But the ancient practice of herbal beer-

Caffe Kilim

making survived on a small scale through the ages, and saw a revival starting in the 1990s. At Earth Eagle Brewings, that tradition is alive and full of flavor.

Corinne and I walked into this downtown brewery and brew pub late on a Saturday afternoon at the end of summer. It was clear right away that it provides a unique experience, even for veteran brewery-goers. Small, but not cramped, there's a welcoming clubhouse feel to the place, that is more reminiscent of a brew pub than a working brewery. Although several customers obviously were tourists like us, there were also a fair amount of regulars. When I noticed several of them drinking from glasses big enough (22 ounces) to make a Viking pause and wonder, "Do I really want to drink *all* that?," I did what any reasonable liquid vacationer would do—I ordered one for myself. I was politely informed that the glasses were for members of the brewery's Schooner Club. Members store their glasses at the brewery, and whenever they come in they drink from them and get an extra six ounces of beer with every pint they order.

Although the brewery does not offer tours, guests can see the small nano-brewing space from the bar. When the brewers are at work, customers can watch some of the behind-the-scenes madness, which results in the creative brews served at the bar. These offerings always include several types of gruit, as well as regular styles of beer made with hops and gruit-style beers with hops added. Because the brewing method is a small two-barrel system, the beers rotate often. I recommend getting a flight; then you can zero in on your favorite and order a pint, or two, or three (I swear, I stopped at three).

Alex McDonald and Butch Heilshorn officially opened the brewery in 2012, but plans had been fermenting for several years. McDonald was already dating Heilshorn's sister Gretchen (the two later married), and the two men bonded over brewing. Specifically, they bonded over brewing unusual beers. "I read [Stephen Harrod] Buhner's *Sacred and Herbal Healing Beers* and [Sandor] Katz's *Wild Fermentation* and decided I wanted to start home brewing," Heilshorn recalls. "Alex, who had done some home brewing years before, joined me."

After having success as home brewers, the duo decided to go pro. From the get-go, brewing with herbs has been a huge part of the brewery's identity.

"Alex and I are both familiar with herbs. He studied herbalism under Carolyn Kelly. My wife, April O'Keefe, is a practicing herbalist. Reading Buhner's book was an epiphany for me; suddenly the world of brewing was a lot more interesting," Heilshorn says. "Flavor-wise the variations are endless. There are so many different herbs, roots, flowers, fruits, barks to brew with, it's a huge thrill.

We also do beers that have both herbs and hops. Adding the innumerable hop varieties into the mix makes it that much more exciting."

Heilshorn is quick to add that the brewery doesn't just do gruits.

"We make some damn good hopped beers, too, that actually account for the majority of our sales," he says. "We have killer IPAs, pales, porters, and all the other established styles you can shake a stick at."

On Tap

They're not good, they're gruit!

The beverages offered at Earth Eagle constantly are rotating, but there always are at least a few *gruits* available, along with creative hopped beers. You'll definitely want to try some of the gruits; even if this herbal form of beer is not for you, it's a pretty unusual tasting opportunity you don't want to miss. As mentioned above, the hopped beers offered at the brewery are excellent as well, so pull up a barstool, try some different styles, and enjoy.

THE BOOZE: Flag Hill
297 North River Road, Lee
603-659-2949
flaghill.com

On a craft-beverage odyssey, one does not usually see beautiful scenery in the immediate vicinity of a distillery or brewery. As you make your way to your destination, you often enter neighborhoods where the rent is understandably cheaper. As you wade your way through ugly stretches of industrialized roadways, most of the time you'll pass abandoned buildings and crumbling infrastructure before arriving at old warehouses seemingly painted in every conceivable shade of gray. The beauty of these trips is found inside the walls and in the glasses filled with their products. The **Flag Hill** winery and distillery in Lee, New Hampshire, about thirty minutes outside of Portsmouth, is a rare exception to that experience.

The vineyard property had been a working farm since the 1700s. At sixteen acres, it's the largest commercial vineyard in New Hampshire. In the 1950s it

Earth Eagle Brewings

was a dairy farm with a hundred head of cattle and a large herd of sheep, but in 1964 the farm closed its doors. For decades the property sat unused, but in 1985 Frank Reinhold Jr., whose family owned the land, and wife, Linda, conceived of using it as a vineyard, and began preparing it to produce grapes. The first acre of grapes was planted in 1990.

After fourteen successful years as a vineyard, in 2004 the business was expanded to include a distillery. At the time it was the first legal distillery in New Hampshire, but many more have opened since. The distillery offers more than a half-dozen different products, each made without artificial flavoring or coloring, and with as many local ingredients as possible. For instance, the **Josiah Bartlett Barrel-Aged Apple Brandy** is made with New Hampshire apples. The tour of the facility begins with a walk across the vineyard grounds. It was nice to breathe fresh air during a brewing tour and learn about a beverage (wine) that is outside the primary focus of this book. After touring the grounds, guests are brought inside to see the wine-making and separate distilling processes. Houle conducted our tour and expertly described the process of distilling, giving one of the more in-depth explanations about the process that I've heard.

The tour concludes in the tasting room, where guests are able to sample a variety of wines and spirits; both products are enjoyable, and complement each other well. I found that a trip to a distillery at a winery was a nice change of pace from the average distillery tour. In addition to weddings, general manager Helen Houle tells me they frequently host bachelorette parties, and it's a favorite hangout for many women. So if you're a guy who's often convincing/begging your significant other to come with you on brewery/distillery trips during every vacation, the Flag Hill distillery might be an easier sell than most. Making this destination part of your adventures in the Portsmouth area is definitely worthwhile.

Signature Booze

Jumping juniper

The ***Karner Blue Gin*** is made with New Hampshire apples and steeped in nine different botanicals. The result is a light, less-intense gin with a refreshing juniper taste.

Strength: 88 Proof

If moonshine don't kill me…

A sip of ***White Mountain Moonshine*** burns on your lips and the sensation follows all the way down to your stomach—just the way moonshine is supposed to taste. This white whiskey is distilled from corn and malted barley and served unaged.

Strength: 90 Proof

Drink free or die

Named for the Revolutionary War hero who gave New Hampshire its famous "Live free or die" motto, ***General John Stark Vodka*** is a triple-distilled ultra-smooth vodka. Like most Flag Hill products, it's made from New Hampshire apples.

Strength: 80 Proof

Flag Hill

THE BREWS: Caffe Kilim
163 Islington St., Portsmouth
603-436-7330
caffekilim.com

As you step into **Caffe Kilim,** the coffeehouse hits all your senses at once: You smell the strong scent of dark coffee, you hear loud Turkish music playing over the speakers, and you see a barrage of color. There are Turkish rugs, called *kilims*, hanging on some walls, while others are filled with a kaleidoscope of pictures of customers hanging out at the shop, as well as knickknacks and oddities, toys and treasures. Immediately you get the sense that you're in for an unusual coffeehouse treat.

Caffe Kilim was opened in 1992 by husband and wife Yalcin Yazgan and Janice Schenker. For more than twenty years the couple has servied up coffee nirvana to Portsmouth coffee lovers while simultaneously providing locals and tourists with a home-away-from-home spot for hanging out.

Yazgan and Schenker were inspired to open a coffeehouse thanks to a close friend who was a barista in Seattle. This was in the early '90s when Starbucks franchises were started to pop up, and many people, especially on the East Coast, were not familiar with espresso drinks. Like other coffee pioneers in New England, Yazgan and Schenker needed to educate their customer base.

"On this coast people still didn't know what a double tall latte was, and I couldn't find a steaming pitcher to buy when we started," recalls Schenker with a laugh. It was Schenker who, with the help of her Seattle friend, researched the intricacies of specialty coffee and developed the place's signature dark-flavored drinks. The coffeehouse uses medium- to dark-roast Arabica beans and puts an

Birth of a Motto

General John Stark was a New Hampshire native and a winning general in the Battle of Bennington in Vermont, a decisive rebel victory in the Revolutionary War. In 1809 when a group of Bennington soldiers gathered to commemorate the battle, Stark, then 81, was not well enough to attend, but he sent a letter to his comrades, which closed with the words: "Live free or die: Death is not the worst of evils." The statement became a drinking toast among the Bennington veterans, and the first part of that line became New Hampshire's official state motto in 1945.

Bar Trivia

emphasis on using quality, triple-filtered water because, as Schenker says, "Coffee is 98 percent water."

The coffeehouse also was markedly different from other Portsmouth and New England destinations. Yazgan, who serves as the main front of house manager, is a native of Istanbul, Turkey, one of the birthplaces of modern coffee and the concept of coffeehouses. His grandfather had a small coffee shop in Istanbul, and Yazgan grew up helping him. When Yazgan first came to America, he spent ten years living in Brooklyn prior to moving to New Hampshire, so his friendly personality has a Brooklyn-meets-Istanbul feel. He often tells jokes, mingles with customers both old and new, and makes all guests feel welcome. From the day it opened, Caffe Kilim fostered the making of new friends.

"We had benches instead of chairs where people could converse with each other, not just among their friends," Schenker says. Many friendships have been made, and there have been dozens of marriages that began with a chance meeting at the coffeehouse.

The quality of coffee, combined with the outgoing, inviting personality of its owners, proved a winning formula. Caffe Kilim became, and remains, a local Portsmouth hangout for writers, musicians, politicians, and amateur philosophers, all brought together by a love of the dark brewed beverage and the warm, welcoming vibe of the coffeehouse. The shop also sells kilims, and the couple owns a Turkish specialty market and importing business that is connected to the coffeehouse. Over the years, the family business has expanded, and Yazgan and Schenker's grown children, Ahmet, Yasemin, and Leyla, often can be found behind the counter at the coffeehouse.

When I was a kid, my family spent a lot of time in Portsmouth, and Caffe Kilim was a regular stop. At the time I didn't drink coffee (what ten-year-old

The Cradle of Coffeehouse Civilization

The true location of the world's first coffeehouse has been lost to history, but tradition holds that one of the planet's first coffeehouses was called Kiva Han, and was opened in the late fifteenth century in Istanbul, the hometown of Yalcin Yazgan, owner of Caffe Kilim. Though some question the existence of this legendary coffeehouse, it is clear that by the sixteenth century, coffeehouse culture was thriving in Turkey, despite some attempts to ban the caffeinated substance. You can experience a little bit of that ancient Turkish coffeehouse culture today at Caffe Kilim.

Coffeehouse Rules

Throughout history the connection between coffeehouses and writing, and coffeehouses and ideas, has been recognized. At different times many rulers have believed these community gathering spots fostered "dangerous" ideas. The French Enlightenment was arguably a by-product of France's coffeehouse culture, since celebrated thinkers like Voltaire and Rousseau would meet and philosophize over coffee. In seventeenth-century Turkey, Sultan Murad IV, ruler of the Ottoman Empire, made drinking coffee punishable by death, but people drank it anyhow. In England, King Charles II issued an order to shut down all coffeehouses after he traced seditious poetry to them. The order was so unpopular that after just eleven days, the English monarch relented and repealed the ruling. I'll drink to that.

Bar Trivia

does?), but I always enjoyed the trips to the coffeehouse. Even as a shy little kid I remember meeting the cast of characters who would hang out there, and I enjoyed the steamers (steamed foamy milk that is offered in a variety of different flavors).

When I visited Portsmouth again for this book, I had not been back to Caffe Kilim in at least fifteen years. I worried that it wouldn't be the same, and that the magic would be gone. As soon as I opened the door, smelled that dark coffee, and heard the lively strains of Turkish music playing over the loudspeaker, I knew my nostalgia had not oversold the place in my mind. Now as an adult I can drink the coffee, and my response is: Wow, it's dark and powerful, distinctive and intensely delicious. At the end of the day, both the coffee and the coffeehouse can be described with a single word—inspiring.

Signature Brews

Going in for the Kilim

The coffee at Caffe Kilim has strong medium- to dark-roast flavors that will leave you wanting more. From the drip roast to the iced coffee to the espresso drinks, there are no bad options here. One popular drink is the ***iced cappuccino***, which, unlike some iced espresso drinks, still has a strong coffee flavor and tastes like cappuccino, just with ice. If there are youngsters traveling with you, a great drink is my childhood favorite, ***the steamer***, which comes in a variety of flavors, including vanilla, hazelnut, and almond.

Beyond the Beverages

Where to Eat

Portsmouth is full of great dining options, but my favorite choice for casual dining is the low-key, **Dos Amigos Burritos** (107 State St., Portsmouth; 603-373-6001; dosamigosburritos.com). This unassuming burrito joint serves up big, sloppy, and tasty burritos that are the answer to your late-night-craving prayers—think Chipotle, only way more awesome. Also try **Warren's Lobster House** (11 Water St. / US Route 1, Kittery, Maine; 207-439-1630; lobster-house.com). Located across the Piscataqua River from downtown Portsmouth, this family-style restaurant on the water has been serving lobster and other seafood specialties since 1940. One taste will tell you why. It's a long but scenic walk across a bridge from downtown Portsmouth, but a stroll that is well worth taking in warmer months.

If you do venture across the water into Kittery, try the **Black Birch Kitchen & Drinks** (2 Government St., Kittery; 207-703-2294; theblackbirch. com) one of my favorite restaurants in New England, this place has more than 20 craft beers on tap, creative cocktails and a new American cuisine menu with highlights like housemade pickles and poutine and duck confit. If you're craving noodles try the **Anju Noodle Bar** (7 Wallingford Square, Kittery; 207-703-4298; anjunoodlebar.com) for an upscale immersion in ramen broths.

Tapped Out / Where to Stay

If money is no object, stay in one of Portsmouth's luxurious downtown hotels, like the wonderful **Sheraton Portsmouth Harborside Hotel** (250 Market St., Portsmouth; 603-431-2300; sheratonportsmouth.com), which provides harbor views and downtown access, and is only a two-minute walk from Earth Eagle Brewings. But this hotel can get pricey, especially during peak seasons, so you can save money (to buy more beverages) by staying a few miles outside of the city at one of the group hotels that offer complimentary shuttle service to the downtown area. These hotels include **Hampton Inn Portsmouth Central** (99 Durgin Ln., Portsmouth; 603-431-6111; Hilton.com). Or keep with the theme of your trip and stay at the **Ale House Inn** (121 Bow St., Portsmouth; 603-431-7760; alehouseinn.com), a boutique downtown inn dedicated to Portsmouth's brewing history. Each room comes fully stocked with complimentary local brews.

Solid Side Trips

As mentioned at the beginning of this chapter, Portsmouth's craft beverage scene is so extensive that even in two chapters, we're just scratching the surface. For dedicated beer lovers, additional stops on your trip should include a visit to the **Portsmouth Brewery** (56 Market St., Portsmouth; 603-431-1115; portsmouthbrewery.com). This classic downtown brew pub was the first in New Hampshire's history, and is a sister business to **Smuttynose Brewing Company** (see next chapter). It features some Smuttynose offerings, as well as some creative and experimental beers. Another beer powerhouse in the city is **Redhook Brewery** (1 Redhook Way, Portsmouth; 603-430-8600; redhook.com). The Northeast brewing facility of this craft-beer giant is in Portsmouth, and full tours and tastings are available.

Smuttynose Brewing

Fresh Air

The bad news for would-be walkers is that several of the Portsmouth-area craft-beverage attractions are not downtown, so you may have to call a local cab company, such as **Great Bay Taxi** (603-326-8294). The good news for walkers is that Portsmouth is a classic New England city that's best explored on foot, without a strict itinerary.

Spend some time at the **Strawbery Banke Museum** (entrance near intersection of Hancock and Mercy Sts.; 603-433-1100; strawberybanke.org), a ten-acre, open-air, living museum filled with houses, taverns, and shops dating as far back as the seventeenth and eighteenth centuries. You also may want to stroll through **Prescott Park** (prescottpark.org), a waterside greenway where more than 500 flower varieties are planted, with great views of the **Portsmouth Naval Shipyard** across the harbor. Outdoor theater events and band performances are scheduled at the park during the summer months.

Highlights

The Beers
Smuttynose
Brewing Company
Free tours seven days a
week, plus an outdoor
beer garden.

The Booze
Sea Hagg Distillery
Each sip of their craft
spirits takes you to the
Carribean.

The Brew
Portsmouth
Book and Bar
A book shop, coffeehouse,
restaurant, and craft-beer
bar rolled into one.

Photo courtesy of Smuttynose
Brewing Co.

Portsmouth, Part 2

The Trip

For round two of our Portsmouth adventures, Corinne and I went a little way outside of Portsmouth to **Smuttynose Brewing Company**'s brand-new and impressive brewing complex, and then we headed back toward the city proper, making a stop at the **Sea Hagg Distillery** before visiting **Portsmouth Book & Bar,** a fantastic bar, coffeehouse, and bookstore all rolled into one.

THE BEER: Smuttynose Brewing Company
105 Towle Farm Road, Hampton
603-436-4026
smuttynose.com

As our tour group walked across the floor of the Smuttynose brewery, motion-detecting lights switched on and off, following our movement. These energy-efficient lights are just one of the many environmentally friendly features of the high-tech, sprawling, new home of **Smuttynose Brewing Company**.

The $24 million facility opened in 2014 on Towle Farm Road in Hampton, New Hampshire, after Smuttynose left its longtime brewing facility on Heritage Avenue in Portsmouth. The new brewery is clearly meant to be more than just a place to drink—it's also a shining, dramatic symbol of the Smuttynose brand that is destined to attract beer lovers from far and wide.

Situated on the fourteen-acre Towle Farm, this facility is designed to be something like a beer-themed resort. Across the parking lot from the brewery is the Smuttynose-operated **Hayseed Farmstyle Restaurant**

at Towle Farm. Located in a renovated Victorian-era farmhouse, it features more than two dozen taps with rare Smuttynose and Smuttlabs (the brewery's experimental line) beers, cask beers, and selected guest beers. There is also an outdoor beer garden, growlers to go, and locally sourced rustic cuisine. The farm itself has a orchard with cherry, apple, and peach trees. plus several colonies of bees. During my visit in 2014, plans were in the works to add walking trails on the property and a nine-hole disc (Frisbee) golf course.

Regardless of whether you take in the other attractions the property has to offer, the Smuttynose brewery is worth a visit. Red and barn-like with a pointed roof and large glass windows, the brewery grabs your eyes as soon as you see it. Tours are free and occur seven days a week. The 40,000-square-foot-facility is one of the mammoth breweries featured in this book. As you walk in the shadow of 270-barrel fermenters, friendly tour guides explain the behind-the-scenes history. The brewery can easily produce 60,000 to 65,000 barrels of beer a year, and has a bottling line capable of churning out a whopping 250 bottles per minute.

The tour concludes with a liberal sampling in the taproom. The tasting is probably the highlight, like any brewery tour, and gives you a chance to sample the beer you've just learned about while talking with other craft-beer enthusiasts.

Despite being a multimillion-dollar facility, Smuttynose is not some investment group's plan to take advantage of the craft-beer craze; instead, it's a true New England brewing success story. In 1987 (back when I was two years old), brother-and-sister duo Peter and Janet Egelston, along with a couple of other partners, opened the **Northampton Brewery** in Massachusetts, which is New England's oldest brew pub. Four years later, in 1991, the Egelstons opened the Portsmouth Brewery, New Hampshire's first brew pub.

In 1993, Peter bought the Frank Jones Brewing Company at a bankruptcy auction; that company would ultimately become Smuttynose, which had its official founding a year later. In 2000, the Egelstons split their brew pub business, with Janet becoming the sole owner of the Northampton Brewery, and with Peter and his partner, Joanne Francis, owning the Portsmouth Brewery. Confused? All you really need to know is that Smuttynose and the Portsmouth Brewery are owned by the same company. And if, after the tasting that concludes the tour, you have a craving for more Smuttynose beer, you can head downtown and stop by the **Portsmouth Brewery** (56 Market St., Portsmouth; 603-431-1115; portsmouthbrewery.com).

On top of Smuttynose beer, this brew pub also offers beers unique to the Portsmouth Brewery; these small-batch beers are always experimental and usually good. Tours at Smuttynose often include a coupon for a free drink at the Portsmouth Brewery, providing the perfect nightcap to your afternoon tour.

On Tap

The finer things

Smuttynose's signature brew is *Finestkind IPA,* a big and bold IPA made with American hops. As the brewer's description notes, "At 73.5 IBUs, this is definitely not a training-wheels IPA." Indeed, it's an intensely flavored hophead's dream.
ABV: 6.9% IBUs: 73.5

Porter of call

The *Robust Porter,* the brewery's most award-winning beer, was brewed to honor the dark, full-bodied ales that were a favorite of the dockworkers and warehousemen in nineteenth-century London. With an assertive hop profile and flavors of coffee and dark chocolate, this beer is certainly a worthy tribute.
ABV: 6.6% IBUs: 33

Tripel threat

The Smuttynose *Tripel Belgian Style Ale* is part of the brewery's "Big Beer" series, which features rotating specialty offerings. This beer doesn't disappoint, with a golden color and sweet-ish flavor that is full of fruity esters. Distinctive and complex with low bitterness, this beer has a celebratory flavor to it (take a look at its alcohol content), and is one of my favorite Smuttynose offerings.
ABV: 9.5% IBUs: 25

You should also try . . .

. . . any of the beers in the Smuttlabs series. These experimental beers are not mass-produced and often are only available at the brewery. Some past beers in the series include the 10.5% ABV **Shebang Triple IPA** and the strawberry-powered **Strawberry Short Weisse.**

THE BOOZE: Sea Hagg Distillery
135 Lafayette Road, Unit 9, North Hampton
603-379-2274
seahaggdistillery.com

It all began on a beach. Ron Vars and Heather Hughes, future co-owners of the **Sea Hagg Distillery**, were vacationing on an island off Puerto Rico. Hughes was quietly musing on the meaning of life while admiring the beautiful waters of the Caribbean and enjoying a rum punch when she came upon the idea of a rum-related business.

Originally, the plan was to import rum from the Caribbean and blend and bottle it in New Hampshire. But as Vars and Hughes began researching this concept, they learned more and more about the burgeoning micro-distillery movement in America and about the history of rum production in New England (the region was once home to more than 150 distilleries). Along the way, the business idea changed—Instead of importing and blending Caribbean rums, Hughes and Vars would make their own molasses-based New Hampshire rum that would honor the region's historic rum-making roots.

They opened the Sea Hagg Distillery in 2012 and premiered their flagship Sea Hagg Silver Rum. Though housed in the back of an industrial park, Sea Hagg is a distilling space with surprising character. The corporate-park feel immediately fades as you enter a warmly lit taproom and come face-to-face with the distillery's logo: a mermaid with seaweed hair, outlined against a haunting backdrop of Caribbean water in shades of blue and black. Rum was a beloved drink of pirates, and this place has a distinctly pirate-meets-voodoo feel. But don't worry; the staff is friendly, and there's no black magic, although the Sea Hagg rum might put a spell on you—one that fills you with a warm craving for more, and like all rum, impairs your basic motor skills and makes you unfit to drive a car.

Tastings are free, and there's also an informal and fun tour that can be given basically on demand, assuming the distillery is not too crowded. This tour gives insight into the distillation process at Sea Hagg, where a traditional copper alembic is used to allow flavors to remain in the still, rather than stripping them off. The goal is to keep in as many of the natural flavors that the original molasses or fruit contributed. The initial distilled products are described by Hughes and Vars as "un-vodkas." Instead of a flavorless vodka-style spirit, the base spirit for Sea Hagg rum is full of robust flavors. This base is then aged in new, hand-made barrels that are custom-toasted and charred. These barrels, along with the New Hampshire seacoast air, help give the rum its distinctive flavor.

When it's finished, each spirit is hand-bottled and then dipped in a wax seal. In addition to the silver rum, products include seasonal fruit-infused rum using local blueberries and peaches. Each sip of the rum provides a taste of that Caribbean beach where the distillery was born, but this taste is cut by a distinct New Hampshire charm.

Signature Booze

Sea here

Though the distillery offers other products on a seasonal and rotating basis, my favorite recurring drink is *Sea Hagg Silver Rum*. Crafted in small batches from sugarcane molasses grown and produced in the United States, it is a full-bodied, clear rum that was made to be enjoyed either sipping neat or as part of a cocktail.

THE BREWS: Portsmouth Book & Bar
40 Pleasant St., Portsmouth
603-427-9197
bookandbar.com

If you could take the pages of this book and magically fuse them into a brick-and-mortar location, the resulting cafe/bar/bookstore/brewing-enthusiast-clubhouse would look a lot like the **Portsmouth Book & Bar.** This used-books shop, coffee-house, restaurant, and craft-beer bar, all rolled into one, is a marvelous downtown destination that liquid vacationers will want to dive into headfirst.

Located in Portsmouth's beautifully restored early 19th Century Custom House building that was built in the 1800s, Book & Bar has a sleek look that honors the building's past but also has an eye to the future. There's an open cafe and bar area, surrounded, but not encroached upon, by rows of bookshelves brimming with used books in good condition.

The selection is full of diversity and, like any good bookstore, it allows guests to stumble upon things they didn't realize they wanted. I found a book about how the teachings of Sun Tzu's *The Art of War* have influenced great generals throughout history. Would I have started the day expecting to buy a book about military strategy? Probably not. But I'm glad I found this book, because you never know when knowledge of the influence of ancient Chinese military tactics will come in handy.

While browsing, you can enjoy a cup of delicious coffee. "Our coffee is from Port City Coffee Roasters right in town, so we get it the day it's roasted," explains Cathy Barbarits, the shop's front of house manager. "We serve simple, quality espresso drinks, taking pride without being snobby."

And coffee isn't the only beverage you'll want to sip while exploring the bookstore or reading at one of the tables. Though the bar and bookstore has the ambiance of a coffeehouse, it also has a curated selection of craft beer that puts other craft-beer bars to shame. It's nice enjoying a quality brew in a different, more chill setting than a standard bar.

You can get a flight of four six-ounce samples for just $8, which is a bargain for craft-beer flights. There is also a full restaurant menu of small plates, and often live music on the weekends. It's the type of place I'd go to all the time if I lived closer, and where I probably would have written the majority of this book, if scheduling had allowed.

Portsmouth Book & Bar   Sea Hagg Distillery

Poverty Lane Orchards & Farnum Hill Cider
98 Poverty Lane, Lebanon
603-448-1511
povertylaneorchards.com

At this orchard and cider house they defiantly call the beverage they produce "cider," not "hard cider." That's because originally "cider" is what *this* type of drink was called prior to Prohibition; the alcohol-free drink currently known as "cider" was called "apple juice" or "sweet cider." Whatever you call the Farnum Hill cider, it is excellent. Dry, sharp, a little tart, with a wine-like quality, this cider is consistently ranked as one of the countries best. You can stop by the beautiful orchard's retail store, or look for this cider in your local liquor store—it's widely distributed in New England, New York, and New Jersey.

Stoneface Brewing Company
436 Shattuck Way, Unit 6, Newington
stonefacebrewing.com

One of the highest rated breweries in New Hampshire, Stoneface Brewing Company arrived on the scene in 2014 and quickly won over the hearts of beer lovers in New Hampshire and beyond. The brewery's motto is "Live Free, Drink Craft." Its name is a reference to the famous Old Man in the Mountain rock formation, and it features an assortment of delicious hoppy beers and other styles that liquid vacationers will definitely want to try.

Tuckerman Brewing Company
66 Hobbs St., Conway
603-447-5400
tuckermanbrewing.com

Located in the heart of New Hampshire's mountainous region, this brewery is a favorite. Named for Tuckerman's Ravine, a beautiful natural wonder, **Tuckerman**

Brewing Company produces big hearty beers and ales that are the perfect match for the mountainous region. The brewery itself is a lot of fun, and so is the area; take in the sights, and take home more than a few beers and/or growlers.

White Birch Brewing
1339 Hooksett Road, Hooksett
603-206-5260
whitebirchbrewing.com

It's hard to pigeonhole this great brewery. The brewery's cofounder Bill Herlicka loves brewing Belgian beers, Russian Imperial stouts, American and English barley wines, and all sorts of sour ales. He's skilled in all of these styles, and generally whatever he brews is great. Beers commonly brewed here include a **Belgian Style Pale Ale** and a **Blueberry Berliner Weisse.** There is also a small-batch series at the brewery that has included, at one time or another, almost every beer style you can name.

Poverty Lane Orchards & Farnum Hill Cider
Photo by Brenda Bailey Collins

Tuckerman Brewing Company

Connecticut & Rhode Island

If you know where to look, your craft-beverage travels in thes pint-sized states will be just as inspiring and flavorful as anywhere else in New England.

Introduction

"It's about job creation," said US Senator Richard Blumenthal (D-Conn.), shortly before scooping up a handful of dry hops stored within a barrel at Thomas Hooker Brewing Company in Bloomfield, Connecticut, and breathing in that incomparable hop aroma.

It was a cold February morning, and the senator had just finished a press conference at the Connecticut brewery to talk about a beer-related bill he was pushing in Washington. Thanks to a flat tire, I had arrived late to the press conference, but the senator had been kind enough to wait. As we walked through the brewery I couldn't resist asking the question that had been on my mind all morning: "So, Mr. Senator, do you like IPAs?"

He looked at me with a confused, almost surprised expression before replying, "I have to be honest—I'm not a drinker."

Now I was surprised.

Blumenthal was at the brewery to discuss The Small BREW Act, a piece of national legislation seeking to lower the taxes on small breweries. Blumenthal quickly explained that he wasn't sponsoring the bill because he was personally a fan of craft beer (or any beer), but rather because he believed the craft industry could serve as a major job creator across the country, including his home state.

The bill was endorsed by 25 senators, but the support of Blumenthal and fellow Connecticut senator Chris Murphy was particularly impressive, given that in recent years, Connecticut, like neighboring Rhode Island, had not been associated with craft-beverage excellence.

For a long time, as other parts of New England embraced the burgeoning craft movement, Connecticut and Rhode Island lagged behind—far behind. They were seen as the embarrassing uncles of the New England craft world, the ones not mentioned at respectable family affairs. And as much as it pains me to say this as a lifelong Connecticut resident, this view *was* largely correct.

In the early 2000s Connecticut, which in the glory days of the 1900s had boasted twelve breweries in New Haven alone, only had a smattering of breweries that served as rare oases in an otherwise dry wasteland. In Rhode Island, once an international powerhouse of rum production, the pot stills had been emptied. The Ocean State was so dry that after Newport Storm opened its doors and tapped its kegs in 1999, it served as both the beginning and the end of the state's brewing scene. In fact, the company was able to bill itself as "Rhode Island's Microbrewery," selling shirts that said "One Airport, One Area Code, One Beer." (Narragansett Brewing Company, the historic powerhouse of Rhode Island beer, is still open, but contract-brews most of its beer outside of the Ocean State.)

But change was in the air. Following Newport Storm's example, production breweries have begun to sprout up across Rhode Island. In 2007, Newport Storm launched the Newport Distilling Company.

Ever since 2012, when state law was changed to allow breweries to sell beer (not just samples) to customers, breweries in Connecticut have opened at a dizzying rate.

Beyond the alcohol-powered craft beverages of the region, there is also a thriving coffeehouse culture. You'll also find world-class cuisine and a mix of metropolitan and New England country charm. Keep your eyes open, and you'll see the sun setting over the Atlantic Ocean in Rhode Island and the glittering waters of Long Island Sound in Connecticut. If you wander off the beaten path, there are many easily accessible country hikes within minutes of nearby city centers. If you know where to look, your craft beverage travels will be just as inspiring and flavorful as anywhere else in New England.

Blumenthal and other senators have come to realize the economic potential of the craft industry in the region. In this section I take a closer look at the joy this industry is creating. But I must admit, my interest is more selfish than Blumenthal's—to me, it's all about the drinking.

Stamford

The Trip

A stone's throw away from New York City, Stamford is becoming an economic powerhouse and little Wall Street. The city boasts water views, high-rise condos, a bustling downtown bar scene, and of course enough craft libations to make any liquid vacationer want to surf these "waters." **Half Full Brewery** and the **Lorca** coffeehouse are minutes from each other in and near downtown Stamford. **StillTheOne Distillery** is about fifteen minutes away (without traffic) across the New York border in Port Chester. All three can be visited in one trip

THE BEER: Half Full Brewery
43 Homestead Ave., Stamford
203-658-3631
halfullbrewery.com

One morning Jennifer Muckerman, the former brewmaster at **Half Full Brewery**, arrived at work to find her beer-making partner in crime, Jon Charest, knee-deep in water. A water pump in the brewery had broken the night before, and the result was a flood of near-biblical proportions.

Charest, a biologist who graduated from Yale and stopped doing serious research to work as the brewery's chief scientist, was unsuccessfully attempting to part the sea of dirty water before him. When he saw Muckerman, he threw his arms up in comical frustration.

"I'm putting my Yale education to good use," he cried.

Welcome to Half Full Brewery, where genius and madness combine with hard work, sweat, and heart to

Stamford

Highlights

The Beer
Half Full Brewery
Good enough to make an optimist out of even the most ardent my-cup-is-half-empty pessimist.

The Booze
StillTheOne Distillery
Offers a hearty whiskey with caramel and vanilla flavors.

The Brew
Lorca Coffeehouse
Stop in for a wide assortment of coffee and mouthwatering churros.

Lorca Coffeehouse

Half Full Brewery
Photo by Eddie Berman Photography

create a tasty line of craft beers that's good enough to make an optimist out of even the most ardent my-cup-is-half-empty pessimist.

Opened in 2012, the young brewery is bubbling with a maturity beyond its years. Found in a residential neighborhood just outside of downtown Stamford, the brewery's somewhat-hard-to-find location might leave you scratching your head and thinking you made a wrong turn. I was in the midst of cursing out my phone's GPS when I saw a sign for the brewery on a chain-link fence outside an unassuming, long, low-to-the-ground building.

On this trip I was with my brothers, Jesse and Levon, craft-beer newbies and unapologetic lovers of "sweet beer" and other extra-sugar-flavored (in my opinion, ruined) alcohol. The not-so-impressive location and exterior of the building gave them pause.

"I thought this was a brew pub; this is, like . . . a *real* brewery," Jesse said with dismay.

I ignored them and headed inside where a different world awaited. You enter Half Full through the taproom—a bright, roomy, and mostly wooden pub hall that has the laid-back vibe of a Bohemian coffee shop. The group seating and friendly feel make mingling unavoidable. Indeed, a positive attitude is what Half Full is fully about.

In 2008, Half Full founder Conor Horrigan had a eureka moment. Fed up with the Wall Street job he had toiled at for three years after college and faced with darkening career options in a struggling economy, he realized he wanted to do something with his life "that mattered." He wasn't sure just what that was, so he embarked on a globe-trotting trip to find a new direction in life. He backpacked through South America, watched the sun rise over Machu Picchu, stomped through Brazil, and philosophized over liters of beer in Munich beer gardens. During the trip (somewhere between Prague and Vienna), the young man with a zest for life and a taste for craft beer struck upon the idea of opening a brewery that could serve as an inspiration to others who had encountered speed bumps on the road of life.

It took Horrigan four years to get the brewery up and running, but now his genuine optimism is reflected in the branding of the brewery and the sunny-sounding names and flavors of its beers. Horrigan explains that his beers are brewed to be complex yet approachable, made with enough hops to add flavor but not make them "so bitter they strip the enamel off your teeth."

These offerings include the **Pursuit IPA,** a flavorful gateway IPA that can serve as an entrance point for more-bitter offerings; the **Coffee Brown,** a rich American brown ale brewed with coffee from the **Lorca** coffeehouse (featured later in this chapter); as well as seasonal favorites like the **Pumpkin Ale**.

The beers at Half Full are creative and have bold enough flavors to keep dedicated craft beer lovers happy, but are not so strong or bitter that they'll scare casual craft beer drinkers. My dad, an ardent craft beer enthusiast, loves the brewery, and now, so do my brothers Jesse and Levon, who by the end of the trip had shed their fear of craft beer and were commenting on the head, finish, and mouthfeel of each beer using some of the vocabulary, if not the knowledge, of beer connoisseurs.

A trip to Half Full is everything you would expect from a visit to a brewery. It offers you the chance to taste some incredible brews and to meet the people who made them and hear their stories. It's easy to be an optimist at Half Full Brewery, especially when your glass is half full of beer.

On Tap

Bright idea

Their gateway beer, Half Full *Bright Ale,* is a crisp blond/pale-ale hybrid that is light and refreshing with a citrusy grapefruit aroma and just enough distinct flavors to make it interesting without being bitter.

ABV: 5.2% IBUs: 17.7

Don't be bitter

Some IPAs are known in the beer world as "tongue-rippers" because their hop flavor is so intense that it overwhelms the mouth with a force like exploding candy. The *Pursuit IPA* is not one of those. This IPA is an approachable, medium-bodied beer with moderate bitterness and a dry rye finish designed to conceal its high alcohol content.

ABV: 7.0% IBUs: 40

Pumpkin head

The Half Full *Pumpkin Ale* is a noble take on an increasingly popular style. It has a strong pumpkin flavor, but unlike some pumpkin beers on the market, this beer doesn't make you feel like you just drank a liquefied pumpkin pie.

ABV: 6.1% IBUs: 45

Half Full Brewery

THE BOOZE: StillTheOne Distillery
1 Martin Plaza, Port Chester
914-217-0347
stilltheonedistillery.com

Like Half Full's Conor Horrigan, in 2008 Ed Tiedge, master distiller at **Still-TheOne Distillery**, found himself looking for work. The once-successful Wall Street bond trader had been laid off for the second time in six months, and as a result had crawled into the bottle—but not in a bad way.

"I needed a job," Tiedge recalls. Because of his passion for local and artisan food, he came up with the idea of opening a distillery with his wife, Laura Tiedge (the *StillTheOne* name is a play on the word "still" and the couple's decades-spanning marriage). Fascinated by the process in which mead (honey wine) is made, Ed Tiedge decided to use honey as the basis of most of his spirits, even though it is difficult to work with, hard to ferment, and expensive. The results of that decision have been sweet.

Tiedge's distilled concoctions have earned praise from *The New York Times* and mixologists at high-end cocktail bars far and wide. The company started with **Comb Vodka.** Tiedge sold the first batch of this vodka out of his car in 2010, but his distillery has grown and now produces an impressive roster of spirits, including two gins, two whiskeys, and a rum.

A must-try drink for beer lovers at this distillery is the **287 Single Malt Whiskey,** a beer-and-whiskey-fueled collaboration between StillTheOne and the nearby craft-brewing powerhouse **Captain Lawrence Brewing Company** (a worthy detour after your visit to StillTheOne). Whiskey and beer are both made from grain, and all whiskeys start with what is essentially an unhopped and (generally) not particularly tasty basic beer.

Tiedge wondered what the results would be if he started his whiskey with an actual beer. When Tiedge ran the idea by Scott Vaccaro, Captain Lawrence's owner, Vaccaro sent Tiedge thousands of gallons of his brewery's Freshchester Pale Ale, which Tiedge then distilled into whiskey. The result was the 287 Single Malt Whiskey, named for the interstate highway that connects these two drinking establishments. The collaboration produced a hearty whiskey that boasts strong barley notes with caramel and vanilla flavors.

In the craft beverage scene, Tiedge is a bit unusual. A former marine, he doesn't have a hip throwback hat or friendly facial hair. He's a no-nonsense guy who approaches the art of making spirits with military precision and skill, and his distillery is equally unique.

It has the feel of a true speakeasy. As you approach there are no big signs or crowds flocking to the place, which is in the back of an industrial enclave nestled between the banks of the Byram River and a hill.

Tours are offered on weekends by appointment only and are conducted by Tiedge, whose time is flexible; he can often work with your schedule to fit in a tour. Although calling ahead can be inconvenient, it guarantees a true insider's look at the place. You also get the royal treatment and a chance to meet and talk with the master distiller, and that's well worth the advance planning.

Signature Booze

Combing the area
Comb Vodka is the distillery's flagship product. It's a smooth, full-bodied vodka with a slight hint of orange blossoms. The honey-wine base gives it a slight sweetness. Ultimately, it's a vodka that turns up its nose at the notion that good vodka is flavorless.
Strength: 80 proof

Wheat week
Westchester Wheat Whiskey is made from organic wheat grown in New York State. The spirit is carefully distilled to capture the essence of the grain and aged in charred new American oak barrels to add nuance and complexity, ultimately creating a soft and smooth whiskey.
Strength: 90 proof

Head here
The *Comb Jarhead Gin* is a nod to Tiedge's days in the Marines and a tribute to those still serving their country. Distilled with a blend of organic New York State wheat and honey, Jarhead Gin is bright and lively, with juniper, coriander, fresh citrus, ginger, and some top-secret botanicals. These ingredients create a smooth and refreshing gin.
Strength: 90.4 proof

Bar Trivia

Birth of the Cocktail

According to local lore, the term *cocktail* was coined in Elmsford, New York, not far from StillTheOne's home in Port Chester. Legend holds that during the Revolutionary War, a local colonial tavern ran out of wooden stirrers and started using the quills of roosters' tail feathers (by some accounts, these were plundered from local British loyalists) to stir the drinks, thus giving rise to the term.

THE BREWS: Lorca
125 Bedford St., Stamford
203-504-2847
lorcastamford.com

As we've already seen in this chapter, unemployment can motivate craft-beverage artists to produce a great product. Like her future counterparts in the Stamford craft-beverage scene, Leyla Dam was out of work. After the economic collapse of 2008, Dam, an architect by trade, left the New York architectural firm she was working for because she was tired of the uncertainty over her job.

The native of Spain was living in New York City, but had grown up on a steady diet of churros (fried-dough pastry) and cortados (a Spanish espresso drink made with warm milk). She had a passion for both, and with few prospects of work in a down economy, she began looking outside the box for inspiration.

"Working at coffee shops, I realized that learning about coffee was a black hole," she recalls. "There was so much information, and baristas were becoming like sommeliers, speaking about terroir, origin, and varietals."

On top of that, making pastries was second nature to her.

"I grew up in Spain and loved cooking, so I thought the natural pairing was a Spanish-inspired pastry and coffee shop. I pitched to investors, gathered up enough funding, spent a few months in Spain shadowing a churro maker, and found the space that we are in now."

In 2012, Dam opened the doors to her new place, **Lorca**, a small but oh-so-very-hip downtown coffee shop that features a wide assortment of artisan coffee drinks and mouthwateringly good churros. Here coffee lovers can refuel and wake up after a trip to the brewery or distillery by choosing from a selection of pour-overs, cortados, cappuccinos, lattes, and cold-brewed coffees. The hot and cold brews here are the perfect pick-me-up after an afternoon of beer drinking. But they're more than just that; they're also a work of liquid art in their own right. Dam approaches coffee making with the same precision and artistry she once applied to architecture.

"To make high-quality coffee is an endeavor that is actually a lot harder than it seems," she says. The process starts with the quality coffee; Lorca uses only hand-picked coffee and light roasts.

"When you have high-quality coffee, you don't want to dark-roast it because its natural flavors will disappear and bitterness and char will appear," Dam said. Then there's the right equipment and supplemental ingredients.

"We use high-quality filtered water and organic, grass-fed milk," she says. "Milk is 75 percent of most espresso-based lattes or cappuccinos, so the sweeter and more tasty the milk is naturally, the better the drink will taste ultimately. I tasted over twenty milks side by side before choosing our current brand."

Then there is the skill needed to fuse these ingredients into one drink. Before they can serve a customer, each employee must complete at least two months of coffee training at the cafe. A similar amount of dedication goes into the delicious baked goods at the coffeehouse, and you'd be foolish to leave without trying one of these.

Since leaving her job at the firm, Dam has never looked back. "If anyone out there is looking to open up their own restaurant, cafe, or clothing line, I say, 'Do it.' It's the most rewarding thing in the world," she says.

Signature Brews

A tad of cortado

One of the customer favorites at Lorca is the *cortado,* a Spanish drink that's made with two shots of espresso and equal parts steamed milk, served a bit cooler than your average espresso drink, so that one can enjoy it quickly and then hit the road. It's delicious and fairly uncommon in New England.

Ditto cortadito

Equally popular at the café is the *cortadito,* a Cuban version of the *cortado,* where the espresso is infused with sugar and then topped with the same steamed milk.

Look out for lorchatas

A *lorchata* is one drink you won't find anywhere else because it was created at Lorca. It's made with a coffee concentrate (cold-brewed overnight) and the cafe's house horchata, which is home-made rice milk infused with vanilla, cinnamon, and sugar. A lorchata is served over ice. It's unlike any other espresso drink you ever had, and is a must-try.

Lorca
Coffeehouse

Coalhouse Pizza
(next page)

Cask Republic
Photo by Noah Fecks
(next page)

Fresh Air

Lorca is located downtown and is easily accessible by pedestrians, but neither Half Full nor StillTheOne in Stamford are in good walking areas, so bring a designated driver or plan on cabbing it. Local cab companies include **Hoyt's Taxi Service** (203-972-0677) and **Stamford Yellow Cab** (203-967-3633).

If you're looking for a great walk in the area, check out the **New Croton Dam.** A little over a half-hour away from StillTheOne Distillery on Route 129 in Cortlandt Manor, New York, this historic dam (ignore the word "new" in its name) is probably one of the coolest places on the globe you've never heard of. It is said to be the third-largest hand-hewn (cut) structure on Earth, and is like a mini Hoover Dam and Niagara Falls rolled into one. It truly is spectacular, and worth a small detour to check out.

Beyond the Beverages

Where to Eat

After eating their fill of the baked goods at Lorca, beer lovers will want to head straight to **Coalhouse Pizza** (85 High Ridge Road, Stamford; 203-977-7700; coalhousepizza.com). Not only do they offer excellent pizza, but they've also got more than eighty beers craft beers on tap, beer cocktails, beer events, and bargains like a $12 pitcher.

If you're in the mood for something more exotic, stop by **Layla's Falafel** (245 Main St., Stamford; 203-316-9041; laylasfalafel.com) for some great Middle Eastern cuisine. Order the falafel deluxe sandwich, a traditional falafel sandwich with fried eggplant on top, which adds an extra jolt of flavor.

Tapped Out / Where to Stay

After drinking the evening away, tired craft-beverage lovers can find a bed a half-mile from Half Full at the sleek **Stamford Hotel & Executive Meeting Center** (1 First Stamford Place, Stamford; 203-967-2222; hiltonstamfordhotel.com). Another nearby lodging option is the **Stamford Marriott Hotel & Spa,** which is 1.5 miles away from the brewery (243 Tresser Blvd., Stamford; 203-357-9555; marriott.com). As an added plus for beer lovers, both hotel bars carry Half Full beer.

Solid Side Trips

No beer lover should leave Stamford without visiting the beer mecca that is **Cask Republic** (191 Summer St., Stamford; 203-348-2275; caskrepublic.com). This true beer bar in every sense of the word has more than thirty tap lines, as well as an extensive spirits list and excellent on-premises hard-liquor flavor infusions.

Bridgeport and Stratford

The Trip

Bridgeport doesn't make many must-visit tourist lists, but this southwestern Connecticut city, particularly the Black Rock section, has a thriving arts and music scene that has become a craft-beverage hot spot. Black Rock is home to **Source Coffeehouse,** a great artisan shop whose coffee is worth savoring. Across the town line in Stratford is **Two Roads Brewing Company** (just off I-95's exit 31). This brewery only opened in 2012 but already is one of the biggest in New England, and has become one of the most recognizable Connecticut beer brands. Although, as of 2016, there was no distillery within easy striking distance, this area is a craft beverage stopover that any liquid vacationer traveling through the state on I-95 won't want to miss.

THE BEER:
Two Roads Brewing Company
1700 Stratford Ave., Stratford
203-335-2010
tworoadsbrewing.com

When two roads diverged in life's yellow wood, Brad Hittle took the road with more beer on it.

The beer lover with a presidential jawline joined forces with world-class brewer Phil Markowski and fellow business-minded beer aficionados Clement Pellani and Peter Doering, and, with the help of investors, opened **Two Roads Brewing Company,** a colossal craft-brewing palace in Stratford.

Two Roads is housed in the once-abandoned US Baird building, built in 1911, where heavy-duty printing presses were manufactured. Now it is a sprawling

Highlights

The Beer
Two Roads Brewing Co.
A sprawling cathedral of craft brewing.

The Brew
Source Coffeehouse
Flavors light roasts with fruity, complex flavors.

Two Roads Brewing Co.

cathedral of craft brewing with a whopping 150,000-barrel annual capacity. Hittle and his drinking buddies (I mean, business partners) saw potential the first time they walked into the abandoned and crumbling factory. Back then, scraps of old metal littered the floor and asbestos still lingered in the walls. The edifice had all the grace and feng shui of an abandoned prison.

But Hittle saw something more: a raw space brimming with potential and begging for development. "Some look at the idle, old manufacturing buildings that dot the landscape throughout New England and see blight," he later would write. "When we saw the proud old U. S. Baird building, we saw a beautiful symbol of America's past manufacturing might, and the opportunity to revitalize a great piece of history (not to mention an ideal building for a brewery)."

A native of Connecticut, Hittle has traveled down some unusual roads. After college he worked on an offshore drilling ship in Southeast Asia. Back on dry land, he earned a Master's degree in business administration at the Kellogg School of Management at Northwestern University in Illinois, and entered the beer industry as a marketing executive. He worked for Rolling Rock, and then was chief marketing officer at Pabst Brewing Company, where he helped to promote megapopular brands like Lone Star and Primo. He also revitalized Pabst Blue Ribbon, "PBR," playing a role in making it the hipster-beer icon it has become.

When Two Roads opened in late 2012, Brad quickly put his beer marketing skills to good use, and before long his new brewery was flexing its craft beer muscles. By the time the brewery had been open a year, its products already were a mainstay at liquor stores and bars serving craft beer across Connecticut. The big brewery promptly gained a well-deserved reputation for its excellent year-round beers—which include several IPAs, a dry-hopped saison, and a delicious Hefeweizen—and for its creative seasonal and specialty brews. A recent brewery-only release called **Urban Funk** was a sour beer made with wild yeast captured during Hurricane Sandy.

My trip to this hallowed hall of craft beer was a memorable one. While many breweries are housed in drab industrial-type buildings, the Two Roads building has a classic redbrick exterior. Outside the entrance is a beer garden with plenty of picnic tables. After entering the brewery, you immediately walk up a long flight of stairs where an impressive taproom awaits.

Two Roads takes its name from the opening words of Robert Frost's iconic poem, "The Road Not Taken." And when it comes to taproom design, the place has taken the road less traveled. In many breweries the taproom is an afterthought—often a small, nondescript area right outside the brewery. While that type of low-key approach can have its charm, Two Roads's taproom is a far cry from that. It is a big, sleek, and stunning architectural achievement. It's an open, wooden expanse overlooking the brewing facility that extends below, a canyon of giant glittering silver vats and other beer supplies. It's both futuristic and throwback, the type of high-tech but still rustic space Captain Kirk might buy when he retires from the starship *Enterprise* and settles down back on Earth.

Regularly scheduled tours are in-depth and more informative and organized than your average brewery tour. Beyond brewing its own beers, Two Roads also does a great deal of contract-brewing work for some popular craft brands, including **Evil Twin Brewing** and **Lawson's Finest Liquids** in Vermont.

On Tap

Ruin-ation
Road 2 Ruin Double IPA is the true tongue-ripper in the Two Roads lineup. Not for the timid, this big hop-centric double IPA packs a double wallop of bite, with four American hop varieties and a light malt backdrop. It will take hop lovers on the road to beer nirvana, but will have craft-brew newbies clicking their heels like Dorothy and crying, "There's no beer like Bud Light."
ABV: 7.6%

Work startage
The workers of the world may have followed Karl Marx's dream and united, had they only served *Worker's Comp Saison* at the meetings. Two Roads's saison is full of intense flavors and lacks the bold bite of some of the brewery's other offerings. This traditional farmhouse ale is made using an expressive yeast strain that contributes an array of tropical fruit notes, spice flavors, and aromatics.
ABV: 4.8%

Word to the Weizen
Two Roads brewmaster Phil Markowski went all in with *No Limits Hefeweizen,* a refreshing and powerful-tasting take on the classic Bavarian wheat beer. The dark golden beer has a fruity aroma and dry finish and is perfect for the summer months. This is my favorite beer from Two Roads's year-round offerings.
ABV: 5.0%

THE BREWS: Source Coffeehouse
2889 Fairfield Ave., Bridgeport
203-522-5662
sourcecoffeehouse.com

Courtney Hartl, who owns **Source Coffeehouse** with her husband Matt, admits that high-end coffee isn't always the easiest taste to acquire. "It's like a person who only drinks Coors Light entering the world of craft beer," she says. "Their first taste of IPA might have them cringing, but over time they'll find themselves chasing Coriolis [a specialty IPA produced by New England Brewing Company] across the state."

And just like a great craft brewery can make beer snobs out of unsuspecting customers, Hartl is working to convert coffee drinkers to the light (roast) side, one delicious specialty coffee drink at a time.

Source is a small but inviting coffeehouse in Bridgeport's Black Rock section near the Fairfield border, an up-and-coming neighborhood with a hipster Brooklyn feel. The specialty at Source is pour-overs, and for them Source uses a Hario V60 brewer, a type of coffee appliance that Hartl says allows the skill of the barista to shine through while producing "an exceptionally complex yet balanced cup that allows you to really taste each distinct flavor note of the coffee." She adds, "Manual brewing gives the barista complete control over the brew process and the end result—allowing us to pursue perfection in a cup."

As for the coffee itself, Hartl uses beans from Passenger Coffee Roasters. The coffee she uses is a lighter roast than that employed at most mainstream chains, such as Starbucks, or even the lighter regular roast at Dunkin' Donuts. "This doesn't mean that the coffee is weak or flavorless—just that the flavors are quite a bit different from what you'd experience with a dark roast," she explains. "Our coffees are inherently sweet, often with fruit- or floral-tasting notes alongside the more-traditional cocoa nut and spice flavors."

Hartl says the coffeehouse usually offers three to four "different single-origin and reserve-lot coffees for pour-over. These generally will be higher-quality coffees that would be too expensive for us to batch-brew. We're able to be a lot more adventurous with these coffees."

One of her recent favorites was a coffee from Kenya that tasted like kumquats. "It's certainly not for everyone, but we enjoy guiding people on their own unique coffee journey," she says. "Oftentimes as folks develop their palate they will start to appreciate things on the menu that previously might have seemed ridiculous to them."

Source offers a full espresso bar and excellent cold-brewed coffee. No matter what style of coffee is being created, Hartl says great care is paid to the region the bean is from, the way it is harvested, and then roasted and prepared. "The end result is a high-end liquid that tastes incredible," she says. "We view our coffee similarly to wine in many ways. That's why we love pour-over so much—it's like the caffeinated version of a glass of fine wine."

Signature Brews

Let there be light-roast

Forget the darker-than-midnight (arguably burnt) Starbucks roast and enjoy these light, airy, and incredibly flavorful roasts offered at Source. Though the specific coffee constantly is changing, normally Source offers coffee with fruit and floral notes and cocoa nut and spice flavors. Mostly these coffees are inherently sweet (in a fruity way, not a fake-flavor candy way), and you don't need to add milk or sugar because the complexity of the brew offers enough flavor all on its own.

Cold-brewing

With its pour-overs the coffeehouse highlights lighter roasts, but with its *cold-brewed coffee,* it's all about highlighting deeper flavors. The coffee used for the cold brew at Source often has rich chocolate and nut flavors. During my visit the cold-brewed coffee was made from a Santa Lucia, Brazil, roast that has notes of strawberry, hazelnut, and cocoa.

Specialty drinks

Each month, Source offers a rotating *signature drink* that mostly is season-appropriate. For instance, one recurring signature drink was a maple cinnamon latte made with maple syrup from the local farmers' market.

Beyond the Beverages

Where to Eat

Source offers locally made pastries and an assortment of tasty grab-and-go options. Two Roads usually has food trucks on the premises, or you can bring your own food. If you want to separate your meal from your liquid adventures, nearby options include: **Colony Grill** (1520 Post Road, Fairfield; 203-259-1989; colonygrill.com) and **Bloodroot Restaurant** (85 Ferris St., Bridgeport; 203-576-9168; bloodroot.com).

Tapped Out / Where to Stay

Tired and weary liquid vacationers can find a comfortable place to stay at **Homewood Suites by Hilton** (6905 Main St., Stratford; 855-277-4942). Another nearby option is **Quality Suites** (1500 South Ave., Stratford; 855-849-1513).

Solid Side Trips

If you're interested in local history, you won't want to miss the **Barnum Museum** (820 Main St., Bridgeport; 203-331-1104; barnum-museum. org). It's an intricate and thoughtful shrine to the unforgettable P. T. Barnum, a circus showman with the spirit of a craft brewer if ever there was one. Sure, Barnum may have been a Prohibitionist, but according to several stories, his famous elephant, Jumbo, was an avid beer drinker.

Another historic stop that's not too far away is **Silver Sands State Park** (near the intersection of Surf Ave. and East Broadway in Milford; 203-735-4311). At this picturesque park on Long Island Sound, you can swim, walk along a short boardwalk, and get a rare opportunity to search for buried treasure. According to legends and local lore, Captain Kidd buried his pirate booty in 1699 somewhere on Charles Island, which is part of Silver Sands State Park. Can you say "Arrr, Matey"?

Fresh Air

If you like public transportation, you're in luck. The brewery is a brisk twenty-minute walk from the Stratford train station on the Metro-North line, which runs to New York City. You also can take the Coastal Link bus to the brewery parking lot from either the Stratford or Bridgeport train station.

Two Roads is not in a scenic walking area, but close by there are some very scenic options. In Bridgeport, not far from downtown Black Rock, **Saint Mary's by the Sea** is a half-mile-long paved walkway overlooking Long Island Sound. It's a great spot to catch sunsets and burn off a few of those beer calories.

Highlights

The Beer
Beer'd Brewing Co.
Small, but brimming with great beer and great beards.

The Booze
B.F. Clyde's Mill
A rare peek at an operating cider mill.

The Brew
Green Marble Coffee
Quaint coffeehouse full of New England charm

Mystic

The Trip

Mystic is one of Connecticut's most beautiful towns. It has **Mystic Seaport,** the nation's leading nautical museum, and is within close proximity to two of New England's biggest casinos and resorts, **Foxwoods** and **Mohegan Sun.** I live just under two hours away, so Mystic is a frequent day trip for me. The small but quaint downtown is great for strolling, and the area has one of the most robust craft-beverage scenes in the Nutmeg State. In this chapter we'll take a closer look at **Beer'd Brewing Company** in nearby Stonington, one of my favorite breweries in all of New England, and then visit **B. F. Clyde's Cider Mill** in Old Mystic for a fascinating look at the history of cider production. We'll finish with a downtown stroll to **Green Marble Coffee** in Mystic.

For further craft adventures, stop by **Cottrell Brewing Company** (100 Mechanic St., Pawcatuck; 860-599-8213; cottrellbrewing.com), **Outer Light Brewing Company** (266 Bridge St., Groton; 475-201-9972; outerlightbrewing.com), or just over the state border at **Grey Sail Brewing** (63 Canal St., Westerly, RI; 401-212-7592; greysailbrewing.com). More information about Grey Sail is on page 160.

THE BEER: Beer'd Brewing Company
22 Bayview Ave., No. 15, Stonington
860-857-1014
beerdbrewing.com

After about the fourth brewery I visited, I started to notice a pattern. Wherever there was craft beer in great abundance, there were also a lot of beards. Every brewery, or so it seemed, had at least one righteously bearded dude somewhere on staff, whether he worked in the brewery or manned the gift shop counter.

I began to wonder what it is about the love of brewing that also leads to a love of facial hair. Soon after I began to deliberate on this important psychological and philosophical question, I heard about **Beer'd Brewing Company,** a small brewery in my home state of Connecticut that was quietly developing a cult following. It was clear from the first time I heard this name that its owner, like me, had noticed a connection between beer and beards.

I didn't expect to write about Beer'd, as I thought it would be too small. It started as a nanobrewery, which means it makes extremely small batches of beer, and doesn't offer tours. However, when I entered the sleek brewery, I began to have second thoughts. When I tasted the one-of-a-kind offerings, I knew I *had* to write about Beer'd. During my first visit I learned that it's run by an artist of beer-making, the man with the beard himself, Aaren Simoncini.

Simoncini fell in love with craft beer after enrolling in a college course offered at the Rochester Institute of Technology called Beers of the World. He began researching and drinking all the various beers he could find. Around the same time, he started to grow his signature beard.

When he returned to Connecticut after college, he began home-brewing and informally apprenticed at Cottrell Brewing Company in Pawcatuck. His friends called his home-brewing operation the Beer'd Brewing Company as a joke, but the name stuck. In 2013, with the help of his significant other Precious, the man with the beard began sharing his liquid art with the world. And by 2015, he had expanded his brewing system and shed the nanobrewery designation.

In this golden era of craft brewing, Simoncini's brews stand apart from the crowd for their freshness, clarity of flavor, and mix of drinkability and bitterness. He only makes small batches of beer and painstakingly controls and monitors the brewing process from start to finish.

Despite being serious about beer, Simoncini does not take himself too seriously, and his establishment is actually more fun than your average brewery. At the taproom bar, there are Mardi Gras–style beard masks that the non-whiskered can wear while posing for photos.

The brewery is located within the Velvet Factory, a repurposed historic velvet factory that is about as cool as cool gets. Picture a mall; then replace that corporate, plastic feel with small-town authenticity, throw in some great architecture and an open loft atmosphere, and you'll start to get an idea of what it looks like. Beer'd occupies a nook of this building. Though small, barely bigger than your average Starbucks coffeehouse, Beer'd is an impressive space. Behind a sleek tile bar, you can see the brewery equipment. It's a smaller version of what you'll see at other breweries; instead of being the size of trucks, here the fermenters are more the size of big refrigerators. Above the brewing equipment is a caged-in storage area.

Small, but full of heart and character and brimming with great beer, the Beer'd Brewing Company is truly what craft beer is all about. It's a destination I first found by chance but return to by design, and if you find that your craft-beverage odyssey is passing through Connecticut, this is a brewery you don't want to miss.

On Tap

To wit

The Whisker'd Wit is a Belgian witbier so good that one of my great (and only) regrets while writing this book is that when I left Beer'd, I only took one growler of it home. It didn't last 24 hours. With its golden color, this beer has a clean, crisp taste; its dryness and high carbonation make it a wonderful summer drink.
ABV: 5.4%

One Beer to Rule Them All

We'd brave the darkest depths of Mordor for **Hobbit Juice,** one of the signature beers at Beer'd. Made with a New Zealand hop variety called Nelson Sauvin, the hop gives the beer its Lord of the Rings–inspired nickname and signature subtle hoppy and fruity flavor that is so delicious, it is what we imagine beer brewed by the elves of Lothlórien would taste like. "Nelson Sauvin lends a very subtle bitterness, keeping the IBU's low so that the drinker can realize all the aromas and flavors the hop provides," explains Simoncini.
ABV: 9.2%

Detecting an anomaly

As its name would imply, **Anomaly** is not your average beer. A black IPA that has a deep, dark color and strong hop and malt flavors, it drinks like a porter with unusual pine and grapefruit flavors and aroma. Bitter and strong-tasting, it's full of flavor.
ABV: 6.2%

THE (BOOZE) CIDER: B. F. Clyde's Cider Mill
129 North Stonington Road, Old Mystic
860-536-3354
bfclydescidermill.com

Readers, be forewarned: This section is not about a distillery, and it's not about a cider house that produces beer-like cider—it's about a cider house that produces apple wine. It's included not for its apple wines, per se, but because of the enchanting nature of where these products are made. It's worth a visit if you find yourself exploring Mystic area at the right time of year. The cider mill is in operation only from September to late December, during and immediately following the apple harvest.

Located in an almost-hidden hollow off a quiet country road, **B. F. Clyde's Cider Mill** has the look and feel of a small Renaissance faire or country village. The complex has several small wooden structures, each giving off a sense of history. There is the shop area where guests can sample and try the cider, as well as choose from a variety of fresh-baked country goods, including pies, doughnuts, and kettle corn (you should definitely come with an appetite). Across the parking lot from this building is the cider mill itself. At select times, guests can see the steam-powered mill at work pressing apples into cider.

If you can time your trip to coincide with the mill's operation, watching the process is fascinating. A giant truck is backed up to the outside of the mill where the fresh apples are placed on an old-fashioned conveyer belt that crushes them into a pulpy mass called *pomace*. The pomace is later squeezed/pressed to extract its juice. The process was once so common in New England that Nathaniel Hawthorne described it in his novel, *The Marble Faun*.

The sight of an operating cider mill has become less common in New England, but it's one (minus the horses) that still can be seen here come harvest time, and has been a yearly tradition for well over a hundred years. The place was established in 1881 and reportedly operates the oldest steam-powered cider mill in the country.

A visit to B. F. Clyde's Cider Mill is a pilgrimage that provides an inside look at the history of craft beverages and the history of New England in general. Even if you don't care for the wine, at the very least you'll like the doughnuts.

Signature Cider

Spill the wine

Hard cider basically is regular cider that has been fermented. The hard ciders I prefer—and that you're more likely to see at beer festivals and beer bars—are beer-like hard ciders that in many ways taste like apple-flavored beer. B. F. Clyde's products here have wine flavors, with a strong acidic bite, and some beer drinkers will shy away from them. However, wine drinkers with a craving for apple flavors will be in a wonderland of products, and able to choose from a variety of freshly made hard ciders or hard ciders that have been bottled and aged.

Johnny Appleseed and the Seeds of Hard Cider

Massachusetts-born John Chapman, more commonly known as Johnny Appleseed, became a folk-hero legend for planting acres and acres of apple orchards along America's Western frontier, which at the time meant anything west of Pennsylvania. He achieved almost fairy-tale status for his kind ways and early conservation efforts, but there's a part of the tale we don't tell school kids: Johnny was a boozer. The apples he planted tasted very little like the apples we eat today, and were used primarily for the production of cider . . . hard cider. For many in America at the time, hard cider was the drink of choice. Some estimate that transplanted New Englanders working on the Western frontier drank as much as 10.52 ounces of hard cider per day; for comparison, the average person today drinks about 20 ounces of water per day.

Bar Trivia

THE BREWS: Green Marble Coffee
8 Steamboat Wharf, Mystic
860-572-0012
greenmarblecoffee.com

Green Marble Coffee, at 8 Steamboat Wharf, is located on a quaint alley off Mystic's main drag. The coffeehouse is a throwback destination that is full of New England charm.

Like Nantucket Coffee Roasters (profiled elsewhere in this book), Green Marble is an excellent coffee roaster that operates an equally excellent public coffee shop, providing the perfect culinary complement to the historic and seafaring culture of the town where it is found. Many businesses in the area have nautical-inspired names, and the drawbridge that runs through the center of town is nearly a century old.

Steamboat Wharf is a redbrick alley with an Old World flair. As you approach, you can see Green Marble's old-fashioned swinging sign, and underneath are tables and seats where you can sit with your coffee and enjoy a good book. The shop is a mixture of funky and sleek, with hardwood floors and polished wood counter spaces, but you'll also find interesting artwork on the walls and painted chess sets on some of the tables. One side of the room has a rack of shelves filled with freshly roasted coffee beans available for purchase.

As far as the drinks offered here, there are different coffee roasts, iced coffees, and the usual espresso drinks. I've visited this coffee shop on several occasions, most recently on a cold, early winter's day when a bitter wind blew in from the nearby water. As soon as I walked into the shop I was warmed by the smell of coffee, and when I left with a hot cup of cappuccino, there was a smile on my face.

Signature Brews

Super supremo
One of the signature roasts, the **Colombian Supremo**, has a full body and moderate acidity. South American beans are used to produce this flavorful cup of coffee.

Double A
The **Kenya AA** uses beans grown more than three thousand feet above sea level. The coffee has a rich, snappy flavor with sharpness and a lively aroma.

Espresso train
The **Espresso Blend** utilizes a secret recipe of beans from Costa Rica. The result is a moderately dark coffee that makes an excellent cup of cappuccino.

Green Marble Coffee

Fresh Air

The best walking bet in this area is to head to the ocean and walk along the sand. **Misquamicut State Beach** is nearby and offers three miles of beaches where you can watch the waves during your stroll. If a long walk on the beach is not your thing, local cab companies include **Wright's Taxi** (based out of Westerly, RI; 401-596-8294), and the **Yellow Cab Company** (in Mystic; 860-536-8888).

Beyond the Beverages

Where to Eat

Look no further than the **Engine Room** (14 Holmes St., Mystic; 860-415-8117; engineroomct.com), a downtown destination that specializes in beer, bourbon, and burgers. Another option not far away (in Rhode Island) is **The Malted Barley** (42 High St., Westerly; 401-315-2184; themaltedbarleyri.com), a fanatical craft beer bar with more than 24 beers on tap. It offers brew-lover-hard-to-find favorites like cask-conditioned ale, and, if that's not enough, it also has great sandwiches and pretzels on the menu.

Tapped Out / Where to Stay

Tired beer lovers can drop anchor at the **Sea Shell Motel** (19 Winnapaug Road, Westerly; 401-348-8337; seashellmotel.com). This small, old-fashioned motel has a throwback soft-pink exterior and a relaxed vibe. It's also 200 yards from **Misquamicut State Beach.**

Solid Side Trips

I usually feel lucky when I drink. That's a dangerous feeling in the Mystic area, because you're close to Connecticut's two popular casinos: **Mohegan Sun** (1 Mohegan Sun Blvd., Uncasville; 888-226-7711; mohegansun.com) and **Foxwoods Resort Casino** (39 Norwich-Westerly Road, Ledyard; 860-312-3000; foxwoods.com).

If you're not in the mood for gambling, visit the holy grail of nautical history, **Mystic Seaport** (75 Greenmanville Ave., Mystic; 860-572-0711; mysticseaport. org). The world's largest maritime museum features a living history village, and includes a working blacksmith's forge and the last remaining wooden whaling ship, the *Charles W. Morgan*, along with various other tall ships.

Bonus Brewery

Shebeen Brewing Company
1 Wolcott Road, Wolcott
203-514-2336
shebeenbrewing.com

Richard Visco remembers the moment craft beer inspiration almost killed him. It was late August 2011, and tropical storm Irene was pounding New England with 115 mph winds. The brewer was working in a small shed on his property in Marlborough, Connecticut, when an intense gust of wind caused a massive oak tree to come tumbling down on top of him and the structure. "It was literally inspiration that almost hit me in the head," he recalls. "The tree brought all of these grapevines that were intertwined around it down with it. I picked the grapes and didn't know what to do with them."

As you can probably guess, he found a use for them in one of his beers, the **Concord Grape Saison.** Now Visco shares the fruit (literally and figuratively) of his near-death experience with beer lovers at his Wolcott brewery. The brewery has a small brewing system, a charming little-engine-that-could spirit, and an intentionally offbeat beer lineup. "I wasn't going to do what everyone else was doing," he says. "Why would you drink another pale ale if a Sierra Nevada is there? Because that beer to me is the epitome of what a crisp pale ale is supposed to be. If I'm going to do this, I want to do it a little bit different."

To that end, **Shebeen Brewing Company's** rotating lineup of beer includes such outside-the-box offerings as the **Bacon Kona Stout** and **Cannoli Beer.** Both sound gimmicky, but they're not. The bacon-flavored brew (it's made with real bacon, not extract) has a smoky flavor with just enough of a hint of bacon to make it interesting but not enough to be ridiculous.

Corinne and I visited the brewery on a brutally cold January evening. *Shebeen* is the Gaelic term for a speakeasy, and, although fully legal, the Shebeen brewery has the out-of-the-way feel of a secret pub. As soon as we walked into Shebeen, we were transported from the cold New England night to a warm European-style neighborhood pub. The tasting room is modeled on an Irish bar. Rustic-looking beams support the ceiling, and it's a comfortable, welcoming please to enjoy a pint.

Shebeen is the culmination of a longtime dream for Visco. The brewer was born in Derry, Northern Ireland; his mother is Irish, and his father was a US Navy man. Rich's family traveled a lot with the navy when he was young, but they eventually dropped anchor in Connecticut. As a youngster, he became friends with Scott Shirley and Mark Roebiger. Collectively the trio developed a taste for craft beer. In the 1990s, while they were in college, the three friends talked about opening a brewery together, but the plan got derailed as they each went in different directions in life. Roebiger joined the navy. Shirley studied brewing in the pioneering college-brewing program at University of California Davis, and went on to work at the Long Trail Brewing Company before becoming the head brewer at Harpoon's Vermont Brewery.

Meanwhile, Visco got his master's degree in business administration at Western New England College. After graduating, he entered the business world and worked in finance. But he kept honing his beer-making skills. In 2012, he decided to make his old dream come true. With the help of investors, he launched Shebeen Brewing Company, which opened its doors in the spring of 2013. Roebiger and Shirley weren't part of the company, but they helped Visco get his brewery up and running. Shirley served as Shebeen's unofficial consultant on all things brewing, and Roebiger, who did mechanical work on submarines, was the go-to guy for mechanical questions while the brewery equipment was being installed.

It took longer than planned, and one near-death experience, but for Visco, the dream of opening a brewery finally came true, and the timing couldn't be better. "If I had opened up the brewery back in '96, we may or may not have made it," he says. "Back then, you were still trying to convince people to enjoy craft beer; now, people are moving away from the mass-produced stuff. They're understanding that concept of farm to table; they know that local and fresh is better."

On Tap

Leave the gun; take the cannoli beer

The *Cannoli Beer* is an outside-the-box concoction that could have been awful if Visco didn't hit a bull's-eye with the recipe. Vanilla, cinnamon, nutmeg, and a variety of grains fill this beer with flavors uncannily similar to the cream and shell of a cannoli. This is the one beer always on tap at the brewery, where it's served with shaved chocolate and a margarita-style rim of powdered sugar.

ABV: 5.2%

Black hops

If a sugar-rimmed glass of beer causes the craft-beer purist inside you to recoil in horror, try *Black Hop IPA*, a dark, powerful, and distinctive IPA. Made with blackened grains, this IPA has a strong hop bitterness, complemented by a light sweetness and aroma. This is the beer that launched the brewery's canning line, and it is one that hop lovers won't want to miss.

ABV: 6.8%

Turbo charge

If you're looking for even more hops, *Turbo IPA* is your beer. This double IPA combines five different grains, fourteen hop infusions, and over six pounds of hops per barrel.

ABV: 7.0%

Shebeen Brewery

Another Round: Connecticut

Kent Falls Brewing Company
33 Camps Road, Kent
860-398-9645, kentfallsbrewing.com

Located on a picturesque farm, this true farmhouse brewery, makes saisons and
other seasonally changing farmhouse-style beers from hops grown on the grounds.
Hype started building about this brewery long before it opened in early 2015—
and delivered on that hype. You can find its beers at liquor stores, bars, and
restaurants in Kent. You can also visit the brewery's namesake, a beautiful waterfall
that has drawn day-trippers and weekend vacationers for decades.

New England Brewing Company
175 Amity Road, Woodbridge
203-387-2222, newenglandbrewing.com

Neither snow nor rain nor heat can keep them away. The constant lines for
growler-fills outside this Connecticut brewery usually start forming about an
hour before it opens. But fear not, the beer is worth the wait. With beers such as
the uber-popular G-Bot Double IPA, and several intensely sought-after limited
releases, NEBCO (as the brewery is affectionately known) is leading the charge
to put Connecticut brewing on the map.

OEC Brewing
7 Fox Hollow Road, Unit B, Oxford
203-295-2831, oecbrewing.com

The name "OEC" is derived from the Latin words for the Order of Eccentric
Brewers, and this brewery is delightfully unusual. **OEC** specializes in making
wild-fermented sour beers in archaic German styles all but forgotten by the
world of modern brewing. The result is complex and deliciously tart beers.
The brewery itself is playfully modeled after the secret societies of yesteryear,
and there's a medieval guildhall feel to the place. When I visit, I'm always left
wondering: what is the Latin word for "awesome"?

Relic Brewing
95 Whiting St., Plainville
860-255-4252, relicbeer.com

This sample-sized nano-brewery has garnered accolades including being named Best Small Brewery in Connecticut by *Food and Wine Magazine* and "Most Underrated Brewery in Connecticut" by *Thrillist*. After your first sip, you'll become a champion of Relic's beers bold, distinctive, and delicious flavor. Try Tropicale—a wonderful IPA brewed with orange blossom honey.

Stony Creek Brewery
5 Indian Neck Ave., Branford
203-433-4545, stonycreekbeer.com

This 30,000-square-foot brewery on the Branford River was designed as a brewing destination. Two outdoor decks overlook the river, 160 feet of dock space allow guests to travel by boat (Branford River is accessible from Long Island Sound), and inside, there's a large tasting room that overlooks both the brewery space and the water. The brewery's lineup of beers includes a lager, three types of IPAs, and a rotating draught-only beer available specifically on *nitro lines* (draught lines powered by nitrogen that create a smoother, creamier beer).

Veracious Brewing Company
246 Main St., Monroe
203-452-7332, veraciousbrewing.com

In the summer of 2015, after operating Maltose Express, homebrew supply store for more than 20 years, husband and wife team Mark and Tess Szamatulski opened this brewery. The taproom has an English pub feel and quickly became a gathering spot for Connecticut homebrewers and beer lovers. Brews offered are creative and delicious. For coffee lovers, they also offer nitro coffee on tap and a variety of tasty stouts featuring this nitro coffee.

Newport

The Trip

The craft-beverage scene in Newport, Rhode Island, is anchored by Newport Storm Brewery and Newport Distilling Company, an all-in-one establishment that has long been a powerhouse in the state. This scene is complemented by **Mokka Coffeehouse**, a neighborhood coffee shop that is full of atmosphere. Because **Newport Storm Brewery** and **Newport Distilling Company** have the same owner and operate out of the same brewery/distillery, it's easy to surf Newport's craft-beverage waters in a single day, making Newport an ideal day trip for those who live in Boston, Connecticut, or even New York City.

While researching this book, Corinne and I were invited to the Newport wedding of one of her close high school friends. I had the brilliant/insane idea of stopping at Newport Storm to sample the rum and beer before the wedding. Spending the afternoon engaged in unintentionally intense pre-gaming was a lot of fun. It was so much fun, in fact, that I may or may not have arrived at the wedding an hour late . . . but hey, at least I was ready to celebrate.

THE BEER AND THE BOOZE: Newport Storm Brewery/ Newport Distilling Company
293 JT Connell Highway, Newport
401- 849-5232
newportstorm.com

Once upon a time in Newport, rum ran like a river. In the early 1700s, the sugar trade was growing in the American colonies, and so was the colonists' taste for this sugar-based spirit. Newport in particular emerged as a hot spot of distillation. By 1769, there were twenty-two distilleries in this seafaring city, making it the rum capital of the world at the time.

Classic Newport rum was made with blackstrap molasses and local water in pot stills, and then was distributed throughout the Western world. Newport rum was also favored by the rogues of the high seas, including Thomas Tew, the legendary Newport pirate. Tew helped to pioneer the Pirate Round, a popular raiding route that led from the western Atlantic around the tip of Africa. Despite rum's success in the 1700s, however, the winds of fate for this Newport pirate drink were destined to change.

First, the Sugar Act of 1764 increased the cost of acquiring sugar and molasses from the Caribbean; then, the British occupied Newport during the American Revolution, and many of the merchants who made and traded rum fled the city, abandoning their homes and businesses. By 1817, only two distilleries remained in Newport. The city's last distillery, John Whitehorne, went bankrupt and closed in 1842, and the last distillery left in Rhode Island, John Dyer in Providence, closed in 1872.

Rhode Island rum became the stuff of sea shanties and pirate legends. For 135 years the state's once-robust spirit industry lived on only in . . . well, spirit. Then, in 2007, the **Newport Distilling Company** raised the pirate flag of rum production in Newport once again, becoming the first licensed distillery in the state since 1872. The Newport Distilling Company was started by Newport Storm Brewery, which had been churning out high-quality craft beer since 1999. The distillery produced—and still only produces—one item—Thomas Tew Single Barrel Rum. With a goal of resurrecting the rums of Newport's past, the distillers make it with the same blackstrap molasses, local water, and pot-still techniques that were popular in colonial times.

Today, a trip to the brewery and distillery—located outside the downtown area in an industrial zone along JT Connell Highway—allows guests to taste some of the finest spirits and beer Rhode Island has to offer within one large, state-of-the-art facility. This warehouse space also has a tasting room that is decorated with polished wood and merchandise from both the distillery and brewery. Nice as it is, the tasting room doesn't have chairs, so regrettably it isn't a place where you can hang out for long.

Regular tours of the brewery and distilling operations are offered. If you happen to stop by between scheduled tours, you can take a self-guided tour on the venue's tour deck, a catwalk overlooking the brewery and distillery that provides excellent views of the brewing operations. There also are informative plaques on the walls that give you the information you'd get on a tour. This self-guided tour is a great option for grizzled brewery-tour veterans who want to see the brewing and distilling space, but don't need another explanation of how beer comes from hops, water, and grain.

As is the case at most breweries and distilleries, the true stars are the products. Here you have the choice of enjoying either a beer tasting, a rum tasting, or a dual tasting. In the name of research integrity, I opted for the combo.

In keeping with the ancient hallowed words of drinking wisdom, "Beer, then liquor, never been sicker; liquor, then beer, you're in the clear," the tasting here starts with rum and then moves to beer. Though the distillery only makes one product, Thomas Tew Single Barrel Rum, the tasting consists of several distinct samples in various stages of its development. It begins with a sample of Thomas Tew White Raw Rum, the rum straight from the still prior to its barrel aging, and then you try Thomas Tew Cask-Strength Rum, un-proofed rum served immediately after it's been barrel-aged. From there you move to the finished product that's actually sold in stores, Thomas Tew Single Barrel Rum, which is the barrel-aged rum brought down to a lower proof to provide a smoother flavor that retains the character of the barrel-aging process.

The Thomas Tew Single Barrel Rum is dark and spicy with hints of molasses and oak. It's the best-tasting drink on the rum portion of the tasting, but it's still fun to taste how this spirit evolves and gets its signature flavor. However, be warned—these samples are high proof. The Cask-Strength Rum has a 108 proof, or 54 ABV, and is *Strong* with a capital "S," like arrive-late-at-your-friend's-wedding-because-you're-talking-with-the-bartender-about-how-*Mystery Men*-is-an-underrated-movie-from-the-'90s strong.

Once you finish tasting the rum, it's on to beer. Newport Storm offers a variety of year-round beers, seasonal offerings, and one-off special releases brewed as part of the brewery's Cyclone Series. For the most part, the brewery offers standard craft beer styles done well, and with an emphasis on natural flavors. The brewery's R. hode I. sland P. Umpkin (ie. RIP), for example, is made with three pounds of pumpkin per keg. Many pumpkin beers use pumpkin extract or other ingredients to re-create pumpkin flavors—or non-pumpkin flavors that are often associated with pumpkin, such as cinnamon and spice. In contrast, the R.I.P. was designed to taste like pumpkin, not pumpkin pie, and as a result you get a true pumpkin flavor—I'm talking gourd in a glass.

On Tap

Rock you like a hurricane

The brewery's flagship beer is its *Hurricane Amber Ale,* a solid session beer with a blend of malt and hop flavors, with low bitterness, mid-level alcohol content, and an easy-drinking smoothness.
ABV: 5.2 % IBUs: 23

Hugh Hefeweizen

The *Summer Hefeweizen* is an unfiltered wheat beer made primarily from grains derived from malted wheat. The result is a refreshing summer beer with a slight banana and lemon-citrus flavor. It was designed to be drunk without a lemon wedge, which often is served as a garnish with Hefeweizen.
ABV: 4.5 % IBUs: 23

Blue in the face

The brewery offers a year-round *Rhode Island Blueberry Ale,* made from real Rhode Island blueberries. The beer has a strong but not overpowering blueberry flavor balanced by just a slight hint of hop bitterness.
ABV: 4.6 % IBUs: 11

Signature Booze

Yo-ho-ho and a bottle of rum

Rather than try to produce every style of spirit known to humanity, the Newport Distilling Company is dedicated to making one item, but making it right. *Thomas Tew Single Barrel Rum* is a dark amber rum with brown spice and hints of molasses and oak in its nose. It has a sweet caramel and molasses initial flavor that is followed by subtle vanilla and oak flavors. It would be wrong to follow in Thomas Tew's marauding footsteps and raid vessels from the western Atlantic to the African Coast, but if you were to do so, you'd most certainly want to pack a case or two of this pirate-worthy rum.

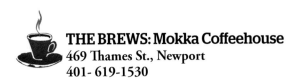

THE BREWS: Mokka Coffeehouse
469 Thames St., Newport
401- 619-1530

When Jack Corey opened **Mokka Coffeehouse** in 2011, he immediately had a problem—a back-ordered espresso machine. That meant no cappuccino, lattes, macchiatos, etc.—or, as Corey puts it in straightforward terms, "We couldn't make drinks." To calm the angry masses (aka, early customers) that had flocked to his coffeehouse, Corey improvised. "I came up with an iced drink that uses cold-brewed espresso beans, cold-brewed coffee, homemade vanilla syrup, and cold foamed milk," he recalls. He called this delicious drink **Icehouse,** and the people approved of it. Although Corey eventually got a fully functional espresso machine, the Icehouse remains his best-selling drink by a long shot.

Before opening Mokka, Corey was a career chef and restaurant owner. When he traded in his chef's apron for a barista counter, he says he wanted to create an old-fashioned coffeehouse that wasn't another "Starbucks knockoff." "I decided to downsize my life a few years ago, and always had wanted to open a coffee shop so I could talk to people instead of being stuck in the back all day and night," he said. "I modeled my shop after the many local coffee shops that used to dot the neighborhood in Worcester, Massachusetts, where I grew up—a place to grab a cup of coffee and shoot a bit of news before you started your day."

The downtown coffee shop is just blocks away from trendy waterside restaurants and is nestled among high-end clothing boutiques, but the atmosphere inside is a world away from the normal Newport vibe.

"We didn't want to follow the herd and go all sailboats here in Newport. No letter flags, boats, or oars," Corey says. Instead, the coffeehouse has a Middle East–meets-surfer-calm feel. The place's unofficial mascot is a camel, so camel sculptures and decor dot the cafe. The rich smell of freshly roasted coffee hits you as soon as you arrive, mixing with the fresh sea air outside. The place's rich personality is a reflection of its owner. "I brew coffee that I like, play music that I like, and sell baked stuff that I like from locals," Corey says.

During my 2014 visit, the coffeehouse avoided new-wave coffee techniques like pour-overs and instead specialized in old-school coffeehouse favorites—a rich and foamy cappuccino, dark espresso, etc. Though welcoming to tourists, Mokka still maintains the local-neighborhood ethos of Corey's original vision.

"We do special secret discounts for our locals, write tabs, loan sugar to people—all those little things that have been lost by the big chains.

We're real," he says.

Signature Brews

Keeping it cappuccino
Thick, foamy, and strong, this European-style *cappuccino* comes in only one size, which is "the way it's supposed to be," explains Corey. Its dark coffee flavor is balanced by the frothiness of the foam; just make sure to wash away the milk mustache that inevitably appears after drinking it.

ESP-resso
Made from a blend of three beans from Colombia, Sumatra, and Brazil, this *espresso* will add a jolt of flavor to your Newport vacation. Sweet and slightly chocolate-flavored, this is a coffee drinker's drink done right.

The Icehouse cometh
Then *Icehouse* is the cure for what ails you. Made with cold-brewed espresso beans, cold-brewed coffee, and house-made vanilla syrup and topped with cold foamed milk, this is an iced-coffee work of art. It's also the most popular drink at the store.

Mokka Coffeehouse

Beyond the Beverages

Where to Eat

There is no food at the Newport Storm Brewery / Newport Distillery, but one certainly works up an appetite when drinking beer and rum. You can snack on the baked goods offered at Mokka, but if you're spending the day in Newport, odds are you'll want something more.

There are many expensive Newport restaurants that offer waterside views, but if you already know what the ocean looks like and just want a great meal, seek out the **Corner Café** (110 Broadway, Newport; 401-846-0606; cornercafe-newport.com). This Old New England–style eatery is legendary for its breakfasts (on weekends the wait can be long, but it's worth it) and it's the type of restaurant where you can smell the pancakes as soon as you walk in. It also offers an excellent lunch and dinner.

Tapped Out / Where to Stay

Newport prices are high in the summer tourist season no matter where you go, so you might want to consider staying as close to the beach as you can. Across the street from Atlantic Beach there are some great overnight options; generally the most affordable is the **Comfort Inn** (28 Aquidneck Ave., Middletown; 401-619-2800; comfortinn.com).

Solid Side Trips

Newport is known for its picturesque beaches and historic mansions, but for something a little more off the beaten path, seek out **Newport Grand Slots** (150 Admiral Kalbfus Road, Newport; 401-849-5000; newportgrand.com). Just down the road from Newport Storm, this mini-casino offers slot machines and horse betting. Races are shown at the venue's simulcast theater.

For a risk-free but more literary side trip, visit the **Touro Synagogue Cemetery,** which served as the inspiration for Henry Wadsworth Longfellow's classic poem, "The Jewish Cemetery at Newport." In fact, folks often use this name for the historic graveyard. Longfellow was inspired to write the poem after chancing upon the cemetery while vacationing with his family in Newport in the 1850s.

The poem takes on greater poignancy after visiting the site itself. The cemetery is located not far from the oldest US synagogue still standing, **Touro Synagogue,** which is open for tours (401-847-4794; tourosynagogue.org).

Fresh Air

There's probably no better place to walk in this area than the famous **Cliff Walk** along Newport's eastern shore. You'll see the natural beauty of the shoreline as well as the architectural history of the mansions built during Newport's gilded age. The walk will take about two and a half hours if you're in good shape, but if you have limited time, most of us agree the best portion of the trail is the one that runs between Narragansett and Ruggles Avenues.

If you need a ride after your trip to the brewery/distillery, local cab companies include **Newport Cabs** (401-841-0030; newportcabs.com).

Cliff Walk

Highlights

The Beers
Bucket Brewery
Feels like a brewer's club where you're invited to hang out with the pros.

The Booze
Sons of Liberty Spirits
A man-cave Taj Mahal.

The Brew
Blue State Coffee
Believes the best way to drink coffee is the way you enjoy it.

Providence

The Trip

One of the oldest cities in America and one of the largest in New England, Providence was founded by Roger Williams, a religious exile from the Massachusetts Bay Colony who named the city Providence in thanks for God's guidance in finding such a beautiful haven for him and his followers. Today, the area is a rapidly expanding oasis for craft-beverage lovers.

For this chapter we take a closer look at the **Bucket Brewery,** a small but superb brewery with a clubhouse feel in neighboring Pawtucket, and then we visit **Blue State Coffee** in Providence, one of an excellent chain of coffee shops that is becoming a regional powerhouse. Finally, we venture about forty minutes outside of Providence to the **Sons of Liberty Spirits Company,** a distillery in South Kingstown that has modeled its business on the craft-beer industry.

THE BEERS: Bucket Brewery
100 Carver St., Pawtucket
401- 305-0597
bucketbrewery.com

After Nate Broomfield and his brewery partners (four home-brewing friends) founded **Bucket Brewery** in the summer of 2011, they needed a space to work. One of the first places they looked at was a repurposed old building in Pawtucket called the Lorraine Mill. The 325,000-square-foot turn-of-the-century mill had been converted into inexpensive loft studio spaces that were attracting a bohemian clientele, including artists, dancers, and yoga teachers. Broomfield took one look at

Bucket Brewery

the beautifully renovated factory space and knew things weren't going to work out.

"Do you have anything not as nice?" he asked as he was being shown around the building. Almost as a joke, Broomfield was brought to a utility room that wasn't much more than a cramped, dark, and dingy closet filled with cleaning supplies.

This is more like it, he remembers thinking.

From those humble beginnings the Bucket Brewery was born. The brewery had a two-barrel system and used repurposed soda-syrup barrels for fermenters (where the beer is stored as the yeast turns the sugar into alcohol). The small but intrepid brewery would grow fast. In less than two years, it outgrew the capacity of the initial space, and the partners opened a bigger brewery with a twenty-barrel capacity a few miles away. The new location, also within a repurposed industrial space, is one of the upstart brewery's biggest strengths.

"I have the coolest clubhouse in the city," Broomfield is fond of saying. And he's not boasting; his brewery is a man-cave Taj Mahal. The line between taproom and brewing space is beautifully blurred at the Bucket Brewery. The tasting tables occupy a portion of one end of the brewery that overlooks all the equipment. Music blasts over the speakers, and Broomfield and the other owners take turns conducting tours. The place feels more like a brewing club where you're invited to hang out than a commercial brewery. The Bucket Brewery "Sound Check" is a brewery-hosted music series where you can hear a local band, see the work of local artists displayed on the brewery walls, and drink generous samples of beer.

The word *bucket* in the brewery's name comes from a derisive local nickname for Pawtucket that plays upon stereotypes of the city just north of Providence as run-down and dirty. But Broomfield and his brewing partners are trying to wear the name with pride and turn it into a positive.

"You don't get to choose your nickname," he said, pointing out that the term *Yankee* originally was an insult hurled at the colonists by the British.

Although just a few years old, the brewery already has generated a great deal of local pride as Pawtuck-ians have rallied around the beer and its brand. The brewery features a simple logo—a lone silver bucket with no words, which says it all, and is an inside nod to locals who proudly call "The Bucket" home.

The beer is equally hip and experimental. Year-round offerings include the **Park Loop Porter,** which uses so much grain that it broke the brewery's early equipment, and a one-of-a-kind stout called the **Thirteenth Original Maple**

Stout that is brewed with real maple syrup. The Bucket Brewery also offers a Consistently Inconsistent Series of experimental beers with "consistent inconsistency," which is exactly as unreliably reliable as it sounds.

The floor in one corner of the current brewery is painted black. When I asked Broomfield the reason for the unusual color in that one section, he laughed. That area, about the size of a small living room, marks out the amount of floor space the brewery initially occupied in the mill building. The brewery's success demonstrates how skilled and passionate brewers and businesspeople can be successful, no matter where they start. As the saying goes, where there's a will (and an affordable utility closet for rent), there's a way.

On Tap

Scholarly research
Rhode Scholar was designed by the folks at Bucket Brewery to be an easy-drinking beer, and this brew hits its mark with a light and tasty citrus flavor and a slight peppery finish.
ABV: 4.6% IBUs: 22

Pail of ale
The trend with pale ales (and craft beers in general) is to infuse beer with extreme levels of hoppiness. Bucket Brewery is intentionally bowing out of that competition and has produced a tasty pale ale that is about more than just the hops. The ***Pawtucket Pail Ale*** (note the pun on the word *pale*) is a very drinkable pale ale with lots of flavor and not as much bite as many other pales.
ABV: 6.2% IBUs: 40

Maple melee
Maple syrup is one of those ingredients that, at first, just doesn't sound like it would go with beer. However, the ***Thirteenth Original Maple Stout*** will give pause to the skeptics who say maple syrup doesn't belong in beer. Smoky and woody, instead of being sweet, this is a one-of-a-kind beer with a dark, woodsy aroma and flavor.
ABV: 6.4% IBUs: 38

THE BOOZE: Sons of Liberty Spirits Company
1425 Kingstown Road, Route 108, South Kingstown
401-284-4006
solspirits.com

It all started with a question: Why wasn't anyone distilling a single-malt whiskey from a beer people actually drank? That was the spark that set Mike Reppucci on the path toward opening his own distillery.

Most whiskeys start as unappetizing beer made with yeast strains chosen for their ability to convert sugar into alcohol, and not for their flavor, explains Bryan Ricard, the manager at **Sons of Liberty Spirits Company.** "All the flavor comes after distillation" at many of those distilleries, he says.

But Sons of Liberty turns that thinking on its head. Here yeast strains are chosen for the flavor they add to the beer, and the beer used to create whiskey is modeled after something people would actually like to drink. Though some other craft distilleries have begun to collaborate on occasion with craft breweries by using real beer for their whiskeys, Sons of Liberty makes using better beer the basis of its business. The distillery features whiskeys made with stouts, Belgian ales, and even IPAs.

"We have a very particular yeast strain designed for each of our beers that is developed to go slower and really develop a nice, full, adept flavor and then push it through distillation," Ricard says.

When I arrive, Ricard, dark-haired and friendly, is standing behind the bar in the tasting room, a small area flanked by aging barrels on one side and the distillation space on the other. I was in the area with my brothers, Jesse and Levon, on a weekday, and we decided to stop in before finding out the taproom was closed. Without knowing the reason for our visit, Ricard lets us in anyhow, spending a good deal of time explaining the distillation process, giving us an informal tour, and graciously ignoring the I-just-swallowed-sour-milk face Jesse, who is not a whiskey drinker, makes after a few of the samples.

Basing its whiskeys off various beers is not the only way the distillery is following in the footsteps of its craft-brewing brethren. Inspired by seasonal beers, Sons of Liberty offers a line of seasonal whiskeys. They include the fall-release **Pumpkin Spice Whiskey,** which is made from thirty-two thousand pounds of pumpkins grown just a few miles from the distillery, and summer's **Hop-Flavored Whiskey,** which starts as an IPA and is dry-hopped. This whiskey has a light lemon and grapefruit flavor that Ricard says is perfect for summer barbeques.

In addition to whiskey, the distillery also makes **Royal 9 Vodka,** which serves as the starting point for several of its seasonal flavored vodka releases (the brewery applies the seasonal-release philosophy to its vodka as well). These spirits include **Mint Cucumber Vodka** and **Dark Chocolate Vanilla Vodka.**

Sons of Liberty is about forty minutes south of Providence, and is worth pairing with a visit to that city or to Newport, which is about half an hour away.

Signature Booze

Start an uprising

It all started with the distillery's flagship spirit, *Uprising,* a stout-based whiskey that, like a stout beer, is dark and bold. The stout beer is double-distilled and then aged in American oak barrels. The finished product has distinct caramel, vanilla, coffee, and mocha flavors.

Strength: 80 proof

Winning the battle

Battle Cry starts as a Belgian-style ale and finishes as a sweet, light whiskey that is rich with complex flavors. There's less of that this-will-put-hair-on-your-chest feeling with this whiskey than with others, making it an excellent option for whiskey newbies. Longtime whiskey drinkers also will be drawn to this spirit's distinctive and unique flavors.

Strength: 80 proof

Hop to it

Attention, beer-loving hopheads: Sons of Liberty's *Hop-Flavored Whiskey* is the whiskey you've unconsciously been craving. Starting as an IPA, the beer is distilled and then aged in American oak barrels, and *then* it is dry-hopped with citra and sorachi ace hops for bright and complementary floral notes. The resulting whiskey has a hop bite to it and fruity overtones that make it the perfect summer spirit. With its earthy, hop, herbal flavor, this is a spirit that can be used as a substitute for gin in many mixed drinks.

Strength: 80 proof

THE BREWS: Blue State Coffee

300 Thayer St., Providence
401- 383-8393
bluestatecoffee.com

Nathan Hann, coffee director for **Blue State Coffee,** takes coffee seriously, but he's not snobby about it. Although he recommends trying Blue State's specialty coffees without cream or sugar—this really lets the flavor shine through, he explains—he admits that when he first started working for Blue State, and before climbing up the company's ranks, he preferred coffee with cream. He maintains the *best* way to drink coffee is the way you personally enjoy it, and that attitude is reflected in the cafe itself. At too many gourmet coffee shops,

Blue State Coffee

people roll their eyes at coffee newbies who ask questions like "What's a pour-over?" Blue State manages to cater to mass coffee tastes while simultaneously offering specialty coffee brews that will satisfy gourmet lovers.

Blue State has two Providence locations; in addition to its Thayer Street cafe, there is a shop in the Brown University bookstore. The small regional company is rapidly expanding and building what one day may become a New England gourmet-coffee empire. It also has three shops in New Haven, Connecticut, one in Hartford, Connecticut and two in Boston. Each one I've visited has a sleek, professional feel that makes you think Blue State could give Starbucks a run for its money one day, but there's also a local artisan vibe. The baristas here undergo training and have a passion for coffee.

For specialty-coffee newbies who are trying to expand their flavor horizons, Hann recommends Blue State's house coffee blend called **True Blue,** saying, "It's a great gateway coffee." For established coffee connoisseurs, he recommends trying a single-origin coffee prepared through one of the manual-brew methods offered at the shop, including pour-over or AeroPress methods.

After a sip of coffee here, it's clear that Blue State is dedicated to making the world a better place for coffee lovers, but the company also is dedicated to making the world better in general. Alexandra Bigler, Blue State's director of marketing, explains, "We donate two percent of our sales each year to local, nonprofit organizations. The organizations are chosen by suggestions from our customers. Each time a customer makes a purchase, he or she is given a token with which to vote for one of the four nonprofits we are supporting at the store, and each store supports four different organizations. Our donation is allocated based on these customer votes, and we support new organizations every six months."

All about the balance

The coffees here range from accessible brews, designed to appeal to a wide audience, to specialty brews aimed at the coffee connoisseur. *True Blue* is the house blend and a good introduction to the coffeehouse's offerings; however, more seasoned craft beverage drinkers will probably want to opt for a manual brew made with one of the coffeehouse's microlot coffees.

Beyond the Beverages

Where to Eat

Bucket Brewery often has food trucks on-site, and **Blue State Coffee** has some good sandwiches and snacks. If you want something more, try the **Wurst Kitchen** (960 Hope St., Providence; 401-421-4422). This delectable eatery, located within the French restaurant Chez Pascal, features a delicious menu of sausages, sandwiches, and other German specialties. The pigs used for the sausage come from a local farm where animals are fed the spent grain from the brewing process at Bucket Brewery.

Tapped Out / Where to Stay

The Hotel Providence (139 Mathewson St., Providence; 401-861-8000; hotelprovidence.com) is an excellent downtown hotel. You may pay a bit more than you would elsewhere, but a stay here is worth the extra expense.

Solid Side Trips

Beer lovers won't want to miss a chance to stop by **Doherty's East Avenue Irish Pub** (342 East Ave., Pawtucket; 401-725-9500). This bar has more than eighty beers on tap (yes, that's eighty!). From New England, New York, and international beers to meads and ciders, this place really has it all. The only drawback is, you can't have them all.

    The Boston Red Sox Triple-A team, plays its home games in the area. So Red Sox fans (if there aren't a few reading this, my marketing efforts have failed) definitely will want to check the team's schedule if visiting the area during baseball season.

Fresh Air

The **East Bay Bike Path** is a 14.5-mile paved rail trail that stretches from Providence to Bristol along the eastern shoreline of Narragansett Bay and passes through East Providence, Barrington, and Warren. It's a wonderful path for biking, in-line skating, or just strolling. The trail starts at India Point Park on India Street in Providence.

If you're looking for a nearby cab company, call **Quality Cab** (401-725-3000).

Bonus Brewery

Grey Sail Brewing Company
63 Canal St., Westerly
401- 212-7592
greysailbrewing.com

At **Grey Sail Brewing**, one thing becomes clear: the brewery is a family affair. First, there's the literal family—the brewery is owned by husband and wife Alan and Jennifer Brinton, and their four kids are regulars at the location. Second, there's an extended beer-loving family that calls the brewery home: a creative team of young enthusiasts, some of whom are volunteers, who help make the brewery work by doing whatever they can. Finally, there's the extended family of regulars (of which there are many) and those beer lovers who, like myself, are just passing through. All are welcomed with sincere friendliness; in fact, it feels like you've stopped by for a weekly family dinner (where the only thing served is beer).

Housed in an old factory, the brewery has more curb appeal than most. Huge glass windows in the front, facing the street, allow you a glimpse of the brewing magic inside. You can see brewing equipment and a small wooden bar, and you'll immediately realize that architecturally, this is not your standard brewery. The redbrick building was built toward the end of the 1920s, and was the longtime home of the Westerly Macaroni Factory. Many local residents who frequent the brewery remember purchasing fresh pasta there.

In 2011, Grey Sail Brewing moved in. After seven months, the brewery's renovation was complete, and grain was once again brought to the building. The first batch of **Flagship Ale** was released on 11/11/11—a date specifically chosen because it's easy to remember.

Tours here are short and casual. After entering through the glass doors in the front, you're in a small tasting room on the second floor that overlooks the brewing space. As the tour begins, you're led down a short flight of stairs to the brewing area. There's a slightly askew, not-quite-right, Dr. Seuss feel to the place. Instead of detracting from the ambience, the uneven characteristics of the building only add to the brewery's charm. In fact, the building's quirkiness has become part of the company's identity. Grey Sail's winter seasonal beer is called the **Leaning Chimney,** obviously named for the leaning chimney in the center of the brewery.

Opening a brewery was a dream for Alan and Jennifer for more than fifteen years, but moving from New Jersey to Rhode Island, and having four children, put the dream on hold until they purchased the brewery building. Now Grey Sail Brewing is a craft-brewing port of call for many beer lovers, and one that is worth seeking out. You can also coordinate a visit here with one to nearby Mystic, Connecticut, and all the craft-beverage attractions in that city.

On Tap

Wave your flagship

Flagship Ale is a golden-colored cream ale brewed to emulate the style of the crisp lagers of continental Europe. This highly palatable beer will appeal to seasoned craft-beer drinkers and more-timid drinkers alike. It offers great balance between malty sweetness and some hop bitterness.

ABV: 4.9% IBUs: 22

Flying high

Named both for the nautical term and for the brewery's co-owner, Jennifer, the *Flying Jenny* is an unfiltered, extra-pale ale crafted with five different malts that are complemented by northwestern hops. Hoppy with a sweet, citrusy flavor, this beer is a must-try for craft-beer lovers.

ABV: 6.0% IBUs: 54

Captain's Orders

Captain's Daughter is an extremely drinkable, ultra-citrus flavored imperial IPA that has quickly developed a cult following. I tried it in early 2016 and fell in love with its balance of hops and addictive tropical fruit flavors. It is easy to see why this beer is so popular and instantly disappears from liquor store shelves and bars lucky enough to get a keg.

ABV: 8.5 % IBUs: 69

Grey Sail Brewing

Foolproof Brewing Company
241 Grotto Ave., Pawtucket
401-721-5970
foolproofbrewing.com

Only minutes away from **Bucket Brewery,** this brewing upstart has become a force in the Rhode Island brewing scene and beyond. With a logo depicting a court-jester mask and beer names like **Backyahd IPA,** you know this brewery has a lot to offer in the fun department. Also, keep an eye out for these beers throughout New England, as they are popping up in more and more states, including Connecticut and New Hampshire.

Proclamation Ale Company
141 Fairgrounds Road, West Kingston
401-787-6450
proclamationaleco.com

With the slogan "big beer from a small state" this brewery burst on to the Rhode Island brewing scene in 2014 and has quickly joined the ranks of Grey Sail Brewing and others as one of the top breweries in the Ocean State. Enjoy beers like The Stalk, described by the brewery as "our full scale hop assault," or the Polychrome, a sour fermented in red wine and whisky barrels. It is located about 9 minutes away by car from **Sons of Liberty Distilling Company,** making it a nice brewery to pair with that distillery visit.

Whalers Brewing Company
1070 Kingstown Road, Wakefield
401-284-7785
whalersbrewing.com

Founded by three beer-loving friends, this brewery has the type of fun and truly laid-back atmosphere that breweries at their purest are all about. It offers flagships such as **Hazelnut Cream Stout** and **American Strong Ale,** along with an excellent lineup of rotating brews, including an unfiltered **Lemon Wheat,** a beer that is flavored by lemons and strawberries added after fermentation. If you visit this brewery, also consider stopping in at **Sons of Liberty Spirits Company** (see Providence chapter), just a few minutes away.

Foolproof Brewing Company

Vermont

Vermont doesn't just match West Coast hot spots like Oregon in terms of brewing greatness; in some ways, it surpasses them. The Green Mountain State is home to some of the best and most celebrated breweries and beers in the world.

Introduction

As I traveled New England researching this book, Vermont was one of the last journeys I made. Everywhere I went, and from almost everyone I spoke to in the craft world, I heard the same refrain: *You've got to go to Vermont.*

I had been to Vermont many times in the past and was a fan of many of the state's beers, but I had never gone on a dedicated beverage trip in the state. So as I worked on the book, my anticipation grew. I heard whispers of legendary Vermont beers like those from **Hill Farmstead Brewery** and the sought-after Heady Topper from **The Alchemist.** Then, in the late fall of 2014, when winter had already begun to make its presence felt in the northern New England state, Corinne and I embarked on a long-overdue journey through Vermont.

Here the local movement is part of the state's DNA. Grass-fed, farm-fresh, and organic are not exceptions; they've become the norm. The state is the birthplace of Green Mountain Coffee, but the coffee culture extends far beyond that roasting giant to a variety of expert cafes and coffee roasters that will make your coffee dreams come true. Then, there are several innovative distilleries that dot the Vermont landscape. But it is the state's beer and brewing culture that make it one of the highlights of any craft-beverage tour of New England.

In many ways, Vermont doesn't just match West Coast hot spots like Oregon in terms of brewing greatness, it surpasses them. A few years ago statistics logged by the Brewers Association showed that Vermont had the highest per capita rate of breweries in the country. Vermont is home to some of the most beloved beers on the planet, and the most celebrated brewers anywhere.

But it wasn't always that way. In fact, like Maine, Vermont was an early stronghold of the Prohibition movement. In the late 1700s, Vermont passed a law that restricted the sale of strong beer, ale, and cider. Though it was repealed sixteen years later, throughout the 1800s other laws with similar restrictions made business difficult for Vermont breweries.

Even prior to Prohibition, breweries in the state were few and far between. Vermont's abstinence remained strong after Prohibition was repealed. In the 1930s, two state residents founded Alcoholics Anonymous. Later, in the 1960s and '70s, as the early days of the craft-beer movement began on the West Coast, Vermont watched from the sidelines. However, in the 1980s and 1990s, Vermont brewing took off and the state became home to giants of the industry

Four Quarters Brewing

The Farmhouse Tap & Grill

like **Long Trail Brewing Company,** and brew pubs like the legendary **McNeill's Brewery** in Brattleboro. These places drew beer lovers from far and wide, including my dad and me. Growing up, stops at McNeill's were part of all Vermont family trips.

The industry grew and grew, and then grew some more, reaching the status it enjoys today. During this research trip I tried to focus on a mix of Vermont craft-beer pioneers, lesser-known smaller breweries, and establishments that occupy the space between the brewing and distillation world, such as the mead and cider houses. I hope I've captured some of the spirit of the craft culture of Vermont. Like so many people I met while writing this book, I have a piece of advice for all of my readers— *You've got to go to Vermont.*

Burlington, Part 1

The Trip

Nestled within the mountains of northern Vermont, on the glittering shores of Lake Champlain, Burlington is a city of unparalleled splendor. Few places on Earth can match the quantity, quality, innovation, and sheer craft-beer chutzpah of the Burlington brewing scene.

Before my visit, I packed six empty beer growlers and ended up wishing I'd brought more. The city has mega-breweries such as **Magic Hat Brewing Company**, as well as more moderate-size ones like **Switchback Brewing Company.** It's also close to **The Alchemist** brewery in nearby Waterbury (sadly, closed to the public as of 2015), which makes **Heady Topper,** the double IPA that is one of the holy grails of New England brewing. In addition, **Hill Farmstead,** about an hour and a half away in Greensboro Bend, is rightfully hailed as one of the world's greatest breweries, and a place where people gladly wait in line for hours.

With all of these brewing greats to choose from, I had to devote more than one chapter to the area. I also decided to mix up the formula and swap in a more beer-like cider house and meadery instead of the standard distilleries. But even so, these chapters only begin to scratch the surface of the area's brewing scene. I urge you to use them as a jumping-off point for your own adventures in the area.

The city also is home to several great coffeehouses. For this chapter we stopped at **Queen City Brewery,** an innovative brewery created by scientists; spent the afternoon at **Maglianero Café,** an incredible downtown Burlington artisan coffeehouse; and then walked around the corner to **Citizen Cider,** a cider house that is making quite a splash in the world of hard cider.

Highlights

The Beer
Queen City Brewery
An intriguing and unexpected layout with a funky atmosphere.

The Booze
Citizen Cider
Serves a wide variety of cider styles in a sleek facility.

The Brew
Maglianero Café
An extraordinary coffee shop in an extraordinary building featuring a hipster, bohemian vibe.

Citizen Cider

THE BEER: Queen City Brewery
703B Pine St., Burlington
802-540-0280
queencitybrewery.com

You don't need to understand the science behind making beer to be a good brewer, but it certainly doesn't hurt. Paul Hale, brewmaster and one of the owners of **Queen City Brewery**, is a scientist with a PhD in chemistry. And when it comes to brewing science, Hale means business.

Hale dreamed of opening a brewery since visiting Larkins Brewery in Kent, England, in the early 1990s. After that trip, he became an avid home brewer, and during the twenty years he nursed his brewery-owning ambition, he amassed more than one hundred home brewing awards. Then, in 2012, Hale put together a business plan for a brewery and enlisted the help of some friends and fellow home brewers. They included Paul Held, who has a PhD in molecular biology and works as a scientist at a local instrumentation company; Phil Kaszuba, who has an engineering background and runs a microscopy lab at IBM; and Maarten van Ryckevorsel, who has a master of fine arts degree and is the artistic complement to the team. Along with his wife Sarah, van Ryckevorsel creates all of the logos and designs for the brewery.

Together, the three scientists and the artist have developed a brewery that re-creates European styles of beer with skill, ingenuity, artistry, and, of course, a great deal of scientific precision and know-how. "We produce classic European beer styles, such as a Yorkshire-inspired ESB and Porter, and a Munich Dunkel and Helles," Hale says. "We feel that these are underrepresented in the local and regional marketplace. In addition, we offer seasonal selections like Oktoberfest and Maibock, as well as the rare styles of Rauchbier and Steinbier."

When it comes to authenticity, Hale and company are always ready to go the extra mile. "We take the time to carry out traditional decoction mashing for our German lagers," Hale explains. They also use their scientific knowledge to alter the water they use for their beer. "For each of the classic beer styles we brew, we get an analysis of the region's water and try to come close to the ionic concentrations present," Hale says. "Our water here in Burlington is a good starting point for this, as it is quite low in most salts."

That all sounds good on paper, but "the proof is in the pint glass," as they say. In this regard, Queen City does not disappoint, brewing a variety of different beers, each with distinct flavors but, for the most part, all excellent. My favorites were the German lagers—the **South End Helles** and **Munich Dunkel.**

Beyond the beer, which is readily available in many bars in Burlington, the brewery itself is an interesting space. As I've said before, as you visit a lot of breweries, they all start to look alike, but not Queen City. The layout is intriguing and unexpected. The taproom consists of a square-shaped bar overlooking the brewery, in the shadow of a vintage pickup truck that is parked on display up above, helping to give the place a funky atmosphere. Asked about the vehicle, Hale replies, "The truck's name is Ethyl, a 1951 International. She spent her life on a farm in South Dakota, and is now enjoying retirement here at the brewery."

On Tap: Got Style

The often-rotating beers at Queen City Brewery are some of the most authentic versions of traditional European styles offered on this side of the pond, otherwise known as the Atlantic Ocean. Excellent offerings include the *Vermont Steinbier*, an ancient alpine-style beer in which the wort is heated with hot rocks to reach a boil—and yes, Queen City brews it true to its ancient origins, hot rocks and all. The resulting beer has unique flavors of smoke and caramel, and mineral notes that the brewers say can't be achieved with modern brewing methods. Other excellent beers include the *South End Helles*.

THE (BOOZE) CIDER: Citizen Cider
316 Pine St., Suite 114, Burlington
802-448-3278
citizencider.com

Citizen Cider began with a book, not a beverage.

"I had read *The Botany of Desire* by Michael Pollan, which features apples as a subject in the book," says Kris Nelson, one of the owners. "What I took from it was that the whole reason for the existence of the apple in North America was for hard-cider production. This was lost with the Temperance Movement and during the Prohibition Era."

The potential of those apples was not lost on Nelson or his friends and future business partners, Justin Heilenbach and Bryan Holmes. The trio began researching what hard ciders were on the market and found primarily a mix of giant cider producers like **Woodchuck Hard Cider** (based in Middlebury, Vermont), and extremely small production cider houses. At the time, Nelson recalls, "there was the macro and the uber-craft, but no thriving craft segment."

Nelson and company set out to change that, and began experimenting with small-scale home cider production. Using a combination of used and repurposed equipment (including an apple grinder built out of a garbage disposal), they produced the prototype for their flagship cider, which eventually would be called **Unified Press.**

"The first batches were absolutely gorgeous," Nelson says. "We were stunned when we made great cider; it was this eureka moment. We really began to dream at that point."

The dream became a reality in 2011 with the founding of Citizen Cider, which has become one of the best cider producers in the country, serving up a wide variety of cider styles, each mouthwatering in a different way.

Where these ciders are produced is equally as impressive. Citizen Cider is housed in a sleek facility a few blocks from the heart of downtown Burlington. The large, wooden, open taproom is a place where visitors will want to spend some time. The food menu is small but excellent, with snacks like hummus, pretzels, and Vermont cheese trays, as well as heartier fare like the Citizen Burger and Fiery Apple Wings.

There are nine different ciders on tap. The rotating offerings range from wit ciders to bourbon-barrel-aged ciders, from ciders with hops to ciders with blueberries. Nelson suggests ordering a tasting flight and making sure to include the Unified Press, "to get a base note."

As to what makes Citizen Cider products special, Nelson has a theory: "Balance is probably the number-one thing," he says. He adds that all the fruit used is locally grown, and that the company makes a conscious effort to be innovative with the ciders it produces.

"Our goal is to make ciders that truly have mass appeal. Whether we're exploring blends, varieties, yeasts, or different means of finishing the cider, the thing we think about most is whether it is balanced, and do we like what we just made," he says.

Nelson credits co-owner Holmes, who has a PhD in chemistry, as "the real genius behind how we've grown to make consistently special products."

Whatever the reason, today Citizen Cider is a craft-beverage "orchard" that is a delight to visit, and a destination that should be on every liquid vacationer's Vermont to-do list.

Signature Cider

Power of the press

Unified Press is the basis of the Citizen Cider business, and what you should start with when visiting the cider house. This is everything a craft cider should be: off-dry, crisp, and full of enough cider flavors to let you know the drink is made from apples, but not so sweet that it tastes like apple pie.

ABV: 6.8%

A cider by any other name

The **bRosé** is a cider co-fermented with blueberries. The result, like Unified Press, is an off-dry cider but with an aggressive burst of blueberry flavor. It tastes every bit as good as it sounds.

ABV: 6.8%

Hop cider

Attention IPA and cider lovers: **The Full Nelson** is a big, bold, dry-hopped cider that even Nelson admits can be confusing upon your first sip. "Am I drinking an IPA, or am I drinking a sauvignon blanc from New Zealand?" he says you're likely to ask. But that oddness is part of what makes the drink so enjoyable. It is made with Nelson Sauvin hops from New Zealand, which have grapefruit and herbaceous characteristics that meld wonderfully with cider, creating the cider world's answer to an IPA.

ABV: 6.8%

The Historic Connection between Hops and Apples

Hopped apple ciders made by Citizen Cider and other craft cider houses are not the first time apples and hops have lived in harmony in the craft-beverage world. Nelson explains that historically, the two crops were neighbors. "It appears that hops were grown in apple orchards in the 1800s," he says. It's too bad the practice died out; I can just picture loading the family in the car to visit the apple/hop orchard.

Bar Trivia

THE BREWS
Maglianero Café
47 Maple St., Burlington
802-861-3155
facebook.com/maglianerocafe

A few blocks away from Burlington's bustling Church Street, near the shore of Lake Champlain, is an extraordinary building that houses an equally extraordinary coffee shop. Located roughly two hundred yards from the lake at 47 Maple Street, this 1916 industrial building has been respectfully preserved as an artistic entrepreneurial enclave known as **The Karma Bird House.** Picture the end result of the coolest Kickstarter campaign ever, and you'll start to get an idea of what awaits at the Bird House, a community gathering spot that is home to a variety of businesses—think uber-hip, non-plastic mall.

A design firm operating in the Bird House, Solidarity of Unbridled Labour, describes the building as "a modern melting pot of multidisciplinary thinkers, creators, designers, programmers, writers, printers, artists, hackers, baristas, bike builders, dreamers, and entrepreneurs—all creating a spirit of idea making and vision that is transforming both business and culture."

It's also home to the **Maglianero Café.**

As you enter the building you immediately get a sense of the place's hipster, bohemian vibe. There is art on the wall, and large open tables where various guests mingle and work. To the left in one corner of the room is the coffee shop, which consists of a small, well-laid-out wooden bar and retail counter. What's being served here, like what's hanging on the walls, is a work of art. Using coffee roasted by high-end producers like Counter Culture, Maglianero features gourmet coffee made by baristas who prepare each drink. The coffeehouse offers the standard espresso drinks, but their specialty is pour-overs prepared at the coffee bar so guests can watch their drinks being made and ask questions during the process. Strong, like artisan coffee is supposed to be, these drinks will wake you up after a trip to a brewery or add a jolt of joy to your early morning.

In addition to more-standard coffee drinks, the menu also features the **affogato,** an ice-cream coffee drink where the ice cream and coffee merge into one thick, almost milkshake-like substance; this is a true summer delicacy. If there are kids in your entourage, or you just want to try something different, definitely order the **Maple Milk,** a Vermont specialty that consists of maple-flavored hot milk and foam. Although it's available elsewhere, I never had this drink prior to my visit to Maglianero. It was so addictively good that I've been craving one ever since, and have tried, so far, to convince local coffee shops where I live to give it a try.

Less than a half-mile away from Citizen Cider, Maglianero Café is the perfect before or after companion piece to a visit to the cider house. Alternately, if you get here in the early morning, grab your drink and then take a left turn out the door and head for the water, where the views are great and there are many opportunities for waterside walking. After a cup of Maglianero coffee, you'll be full of energy.

Signature Brews

Pour house

As I mentioned earlier, all the espresso drinks here are excellent, but the specialty is the *pour-overs*. Guests can choose from a variety of beans with varying flavor profiles, and for those not sure what they want, the baristas will explain the flavors of each bean. In defiance of the high-end coffee gods, I openly enjoy cream or milk in my coffee, but even I recommend taking a few sips of your pour-over before adding cream.

Maple man

You can't leave Maglianero without trying the *Maple Milk.* I know, I know, this is a great artisan coffee shop and I'm recommending a version of steamed milk; however, this drink is excellent, and the type of thing that's hard to find outside of Vermont. It's the perfect dessert drink, so do yourself a favor and give it a try.

Beyond the Beverages

Where to Eat

Think of food in Vermont and you think of fresh pies, pancakes, farm-fresh cheese and produce—a holy land of comfort food. Burlington's culinary landscape does not disappoint, delivering all this and then some, and good beer is available almost everywhere. Non-beer bars and standard restaurants in Burlington offer more quality selections than beer bars elsewhere. As for Burlington beer bars, well, they put those in most other parts of the country to shame. Most bars and restaurants within Burlington, and elsewhere in Vermont, offer sample-size glasses of each of their beers, which allows you to try more beers without getting loaded . . . or, at least without getting *as* loaded.

Start your day off with breakfast at the **Penny Cluse Café** (169 Cherry St., Burlington; 802-651-8834; pennycluse.com). The breakfast here is one of the best in all of New England—or anywhere, for that matter—and it has a great on-tap beer selection. Normally I don't recommend drinking before noon, but hey, you're on vacation, so why not, as long as you pace yourself. Try the whole-wheat pancakes; soft but not mushy, with a golden-brown color, they pair well with a sample-size brewski from Citizen Cider or Queen City Brewery, both of which often are available on tap at the café.

For lunch visit **American Flatbread** (115 St. Paul St., Burlington; 802-861-2999; americanflatbread.com), purveyors of finely crafted flatbread that looks like pizza but tastes different. Because this is Burlington, the restaurant also houses the **Zero Gravity Craft Brewery** (zerogravitybeer.com) and offers brew pub-style beers, as well as a selection of beer from other breweries in Vermont and beyond.

For dinner look no further than **The Farmhouse Tap & Grill** (160 Bank St., Burlington; 802-859-0888; farmhousetg.com), a farm-to-table gastropub and beer bar with locally sourced ingredients. Try the Vermont cheese platter (your waiter can suggest beer and cheese pairings), and dig into one of the restaurant's signature burgers made with local meat. The beer list is extensive, and in addition to superb offerings from breweries across the nation, and sometimes the world, several tap lines are devoted to the many great breweries found in Vermont. There are generally several hard-to-find beers from **Hill Farmstead Brewery** that you will definitely want to try. A stop here provides a good opportunity to sample beer from some of the breweries you don't get a chance to visit.

Tapped Out / Where to Stay
You can stay downtown at the **Hotel Vermont** (41 Cherry St., Burlington; 855-650-0080; hotelvt.com), a rustic hotel with a hip modern vibe, or the **Marriott Burlington Courtyard Harbor** (25 Cherry St., Burlington; 802-864-4700; marriott.com).

Solid Side Trips
Amid your craft-beverage explorations you'll want to set aside some time to explore **Church Street Marketplace** (located along Church Street, between Pearl and Main Streets in

Fresh Air

There are plenty of walking options in downtown Burlington, but if you want something more than a leisurely stroll through the shops on Church Street, follow gravity and let the sloping streets of the city carry you down toward the glittering waters of Lake Champlain. Here you'll find the **Burlington Bike Path** (btvbikepath.com; for GPS purposes, use the address of the ECHO Lake Aquarium and Science Center, 1 College St., Burlington). Completed in the 1980s, this approximately 7.5-mile path is one of the oldest rail trails in New England, and remains one of the most beautiful. It runs from the southern end of Burlington at Oakledge Park to the northern end at the Winooski River, where it connects via a bike-path bridge to the **Colchester Bike Path**. Along the way it hugs the banks of Lake Champlain, offering spectacular views of the water and the towering Adirondack Mountains to the west.

If you're not in the mood for a waterside walk and want to get back to your hotel or to a brewery that's not downtown, try the environmentally friendly and reliable **Green Cab Vermont** (802-864-2424; greencabvt.com).

Burlington; churchstmarketplace.com). Traffic is closed on Church Street, and the downtown square is full of exquisite historic buildings, shops, and restaurants, and frequently street performers. The area also has many high-end shopping chains that provide the perfect opportunity to earn some extra credit with the significant other you've dragged on *another* craft-beverage trip (wait— I'm talking about myself here).

To satisfy your sweet-tooth cravings and learn about the art of making chocolate in the process, visit **Lake Champlain Chocolates** (750 Pine St., Burlington; 1-800-465-5909; lakechamplainchocolates.com). Tours are given regularly. There are no dancing Oompa Loompas, but the tour does include free chocolate samples.

Speaking of a sweet tooth, just outside of Burlington you'll find the iconic Vermont ice-cream factory, **Ben & Jerry's** (1281 Waterbury-Stowe Road, Waterbury; 866-258-6877; benjerry.com). The tours at this ice-cream wonderland last about 30 minutes, and there's a full-service scoop shop with all your favorite flavors, along with experimental new flavors that potentially could be offered nationally one day.

Lake Champlain Chocolate

Burlington, Part 2

The Trip

For round two of my Burlington visit, I enjoyed a coffee at **Uncommon Grounds Coffee and Tea** in the heart of downtown Burlington, and then headed north to neighboring Winooski to check out **Four Quarters Brewing,** an excellent small brewery, and nearby **Groennfell Meadery,** a craft meadery with a quirky, visitor-friendly vibe.

THE BEER: Four Quarters Brewing
150 West Canal, Suite 1, Winooski
fourquartersbrewing.com

Opening a new brewery in the Burlington area seems a little like moving to Italy to open an Italian restaurant. Not only are there lots of breweries in the region, but there are lots of *great* breweries. To the pessimist, adding to that scene seems unnecessary at best and foolhardy at worst. Yet in 2014 Brian Eckert defied the doubters and boldly went where many brewers have gone before by adding his humble nanobrewery, **Four Quarters Brewing,** to the Vermont brewing world. Instead of being swallowed up and lost in the ocean of craft beer pouring out of the state, Eckert's creative beers rose to the crest of the region's craft beverage world. Before it had been open a year, Four Quarters Brewing was becoming well-known in local circles and by aficionados of Vermont beer far and wide.

Shortly before my trip to Burlington, I heard about Four Quarters Brewing from Dan Carlucci, a musician friend with a passion for craft beer. I wanted to check it out because it sounded interesting, but I didn't anticipate including it in this book until I tried some of the beer for myself.

Highlights

The Beer
Four Quarters Brewing
Beers are inspired by a mixture of Belgian and American traditions.

The Booze
Groennfell Meadery
Modern mead inspired by ancient brews and Norse mythology.

The Brew
Uncommon Grounds
Artisan coffee served in a festive atmosphere.

Four Quarters Brewing

Eckert is fascinated by the connection between beer, religion, and the monks who popularized Belgian brewing. The beers he offers are inspired by a mixture of Belgian and American traditions, and he brews them with the focus and devotion of a holy man. The result is a destination that has everything I love about a small craft brewery. The beers are creative and unusual with complex flavors that linger on your tongue, each new release you read about makes your mouth water, and when you leave, no matter how many growlers you fill, you wish you had left with more beer. Eckert is also fascinated by astronomy and it shows both in the brewery's name (inspired by the four cycles, or quarters, of the moon) and beer names like Ursa Major (The Great Bear, or Big Dipper constellation).

Located in the central Winooski business district right outside downtown, Four Quarters Brewing has a small brewery and taproom that have a garage-band, mad-scientist-basement-lab feel.

There was an outdoor festival with live music at the brewery the day I visited, and Eckert was behind the bar, serving customers. Despite the crowd, he made time to speak with me and other customers, explaining the ingredients and brewing process of the various beers he was serving. Eckert hopes to expand the brewery and maybe one day offer food, but he's not looking to become a mega-brewery. In the fall of 2014 he celebrated his first outside account by posting a photo of himself, delivering that first keg to a local restaurant on foot with a hand truck.

By the time I left Four Quarters Brewing, I knew it would be in this book. I also realized that, despite my initial skepticism, there was indeed room for at least one more great brewery in Vermont.

Bar Trivia

Historic Bar Trivia: IPA Creation Myths

The story told and retold in beer halls and breweries, goes something like this: India Pale Ale, the most popular American craft-beer, was born on the long voyage between India and England. Because of the length of the trip, a beer with more alcohol and hops was needed so it wouldn't spoil. As a result India Pale Ales or IPAs were developed in the 1700s and 1800s. It's a good story, but isn't entirely true. While it's true that by 1822 more aggressively hopped pale ales began to be brewed for the Indian market, they were not higher in alcohol content, and they were not developed to avoid spoiling on long trips. Some theories propose that IPAs were better for the hot climate of India, and that its strong flavors paired better with the intense spices of Indian cuisine. Whatever the reason, the style became popular in England as well as India, and made its way to the colonists in America, where the American IPA evolved into a far more hop-centric beast than its tamer, less-bitter cousins back in the Old Country.

On Tap

Eckert constantly rotates many of his offerings, and whatever is available is sure to be good. However, keep a look out for the following beers.

Magnum opus Opus Dei, from the Latin for "the work of God," is a bold name for an excellent beer that is a Belgian-style *patersbier* ("father's beer"). Traditionally this style of beer was low in alcohol content and brewed by monks to be consumed at the abbey. Eckert's version is sessionable and delicious.

ABV: 4%

Saisons, Sours and More
Four Quarters offers a constantly changing assortment of great beers in the Belgian tradition ranging from sours to saisons to more hop-forward beers. Though this changing lineup makes high-lighting select beers difficult, it makes each visit to the brewery a unique and rewarding experience.

856 Hercules Drive, Suite 20, Colchester
802-497-2345
groennfell.com

As the door opens to **Groennfell Meadery,** Ricky Klein, mead maker and owner, welcomes us in grandiose fashion. "Come, drink with me," he proclaims with the air of a Shakespearean actor.

Corinne and I make our way inside. It's the middle of a busy touring day for us that has already included stops at three other hot spots in the area, but the vibe here quickly sets it apart. The meadery is found within a common-enough-looking corporate park, in an equally common-looking warehouse-type space, but the decorations are anything but common. The taproom is in one corner of the brewing space and has enough quirk to fill a Viking warship. There is a bin filled with juggling paraphernalia, books filled with Old English riddles and jokes, and an assortment of items that seem borrowed from the set of *Game of Thrones.*

Then there's Klein, who owns the place with his wife Kelly. Tall and slim, Klein towers over most of his customers, but has the friendly, showman persona of a Renaissance Faire court jester combined with the smarts of a classics professor.

A fascination with Norse mythology led Klein to study for a time in Denmark and fueled a self-described obsession with mead. Many cultures have made various forms of mead, and some argue that ambrosia, the drink (or food) of the gods in Greek mythology, actually was natural mead made when rainwater mixed with honey and fermented. In Ethiopia, Jews make a form of honey wine called *tej* that traditionally was drunk on the Sabbath. In the Norse lands, mead was second to none. Norse warriors who died valiantly in battle believed they would be served mead in Valhalla, and the gods themselves are often depicted enjoying this honey drink.

Klein is inspired by the drink of the gods of old. The meadery's name, Groennfell, is Old Norse for "Vermont," and one of the signature meads is **Valkyrie's Choice,** named for the beautiful women-warrior servants of the god Odin. According to lore, the Valkyries brought mead to slain warriors in the halls of Valhalla. Klein's mead, however, probably isn't exactly what the ancient gods or Vikings had in mind. "We can be reasonably certain of two things: My mead is clearer and bubblier than what could, or would, have been produced before the Industrial Revolution," he says.

Many modern mead makers create a honey wine that bears little resemblance to beer, often is expensive, and can be so sweet that Klein jokingly says it tastes like vodka mixed with Honey Nut Cheerios. Klein went in a different direction with his mead, creating a less-sweet beverage modeled on hard cider. "We focus more on craft meads, a reasonably priced product that's dry, lightly carbonated, and interesting enough to drink every day," he says. "What we often tell people is that 'our mead is as much like a beer or cider as a craft cider is like a craft beer; not identical, but definitely in the same extended family.'"

Bar Trivia

Cancel the Honeymoon

There's a story often repeated at many meaderies and on their websites about the origins of the word *honeymoon*. It goes something like this: Newly married couples were traditionally given enough mead (honey) to last a month (moon). It sounds reasonable enough, but there's just one problem: There is no proof, like, at all. "Despite what other meadery owners, 'fun facts about mead pages,' and ill-informed tour guides will tell you, the term *honeymoon* has absolutely, positively, no relationship with mead," Klein explains. "That's spurious folk etymology at best, purposeful marketing duplicity at worst." Nevertheless, as he happily adds, mead remains an excellent drink to enjoy on your honeymoon.

That's a fair description. The meadery offers various meads, each with distinct flavors that also share some common characteristics, including a beer-like appearance with a more seltzer-like level of carbonation and consistency, as well as a slightly moldy aftertaste that is far more pleasant than it sounds. The meads are not overly sweet but have an intriguing honey flavor. Groennfell mead is like a sour beer in the reaction it prompts: While it's not for everyone, it's hugely appealing and often addictive to those who like it.

In addition to a regular line of different meads, Klein makes a special small batch of experimental mead each week that is offered to guests at the meadery's Firkin Fridays series. Klein also regularly offers informal and entertaining tours that are conducted when time and interest allow.

A trip here is an fascinating walk inside the world of modern mead. While I'd rather not die in battle, I wouldn't be as upset if my spirit was greeted by a Valkyrie carrying a growler or two from the Groennfell Meadery.

Signature Mead

Valhalla, I am coming
Named for the mythical women warriors under Odin's command who led slain warriors to Valhalla and served them copious amounts of mead, *Valkyrie's Choice* pours pale gold and is strong with a dry, non-sweet honey flavor.
ABV: 9.2%

Fenberry Draught is a dry cranberry mead that balances the tartness of cranberries with the mead's honey flavors. Not sweet but not subtle either, this drink is described as akin to "swimming in a cranberry bog with a beehive under each arm," a drinking experience that's more fun than it might sound.
ABV: 5.2%

The *Winter Warmer Mead* is a seasonal mead based on an eighteenth-century recipe and brewed with cinnamon, cloves, orange, and brandy. The result is a delicious spiced mead with a high alcohol content designed to keep you warm in the snow.
ABV: 10.1%

Warm mead up

Berry, berry good

THE BREWS: Uncommon Grounds Coffee and Tea
42 Church St., Burlington
802-865-6227
ugvermont.com

One of the delights of exploring Burlington is the festive atmosphere that stretches down the four blocks of Church Street between Main and Pearl Streets. Here traffic is closed and pedestrians can wander freely among storefronts and street performers without fear of cars.

Among the must-see/taste attractions of Church Street is **Uncommon Grounds Coffee and Tea,** a cafe with a crossover European and New England charm. Passing this coffeehouse in the street, more experienced and jaded travelers might eye the storefront skeptically. It has a pun in its title, not usually a good sign for a coffeehouse, and its prominent storefront in the city's most highly trafficked area looks like a tourist trap from the outside. It's the type of prime location where a business could conceivably thrive regardless of the quality of its offerings; you know, like those awful waterside restaurants we've all visited.

When you walk in, a line of tourists often stands between you and the register; after all, this is the obvious downtown Burlington coffee choice, the one you normally find if you don't explore the back alleys and seek out the advice of the local beverage elite. In this case, the obvious choice also happens to be a great one. Uncommon Grounds churns out accessible but artisan coffee products arguably as good as any hole-in-the-wall coffeehouse destination you're going to find.

As soon as you enter, your senses are greeted by the smell of freshly roasted coffee. The space is long and narrow, with the counter at one end and tables at the other. Behind the counter are various coffees and teas from which to choose, with skilled baristas expertly preparing delicious espresso drinks. Excellent pour-overs are offered, but unlike at many new artisan coffeehouses, they are not the main attraction. The pour-overs are prepared slowly and meticulously, so you'll have to wait, and so will those in line behind you (sorry, folks!), but it's worth it.

Regardless of what you order, you can take your drink and find a seat in the shop or sip it as you wander through the outdoor expanse of Church Street. It's an experience so truly exemplary of New England, you might feel like you're inside a postcard for the region, and, like those pictured, odds are you'll be smiling.

Signature Brews

When it rains, it pours

Although **pour-overs** are not the main specialty here, they are done exceptionally well. Pick a coffee that appeals to your tastes, ask for a pour-over, and then sit back and prepare to enjoy a great cup of coffee.

Grounds to go

While at the store you can pick up some of the coffeehouse's freshly roasted coffee, or you can order it online if you desire more after your trip. Varieties include the ***Colombia Sierra Nevada,*** which has notes of mellow citrus, orange, lemon, and dry white wine.

Rooting for root beer

On tap, literally, at this coffeehouse is root beer made by the Burlington-based ***Rookie's Root Beer.*** Coming straight from the draught line, the soda is thick and foamy, like real beer, and it's one of the best root beers you're ever going to enjoy—fizzy and creamy. On my second trip to this coffeehouse I couldn't resist, and had to "double-fist it" by ordering a pour-over and a glass of root beer.

Highlights

The Beer
Long Trail
Brewing Co.
An impressive German-inspired brewery complete with a beer hall.

The Booze
Vermont Spirits
Offers an unusual vodka that uses sugar from cow's milk in the distillery process.

Quechee and Bridgewater Corners

The Trip

In the wilderness of central Vermont, amid the wooded hills and rolling farm pastures, travellers come upon a craft-beverage oasis in Bridgewater Corners and the area around White River Junction and Quechee (both villages of Hartford). First, I stopped at the **Long Trail Brewing Company,** a legendary Vermont purveyor of fine ales, and then it was on to **Vermont Spirits,** a pioneering micro-distiller with innovative products. Along the way I took in views of the **Quechee Gorge,** walked on the *actual* **Long Trail,** which inspired the brewery, and enjoyed some fine Vermont country dining. Although this chapter does not feature a coffeehouse, there are more than enough liquid attractions in the area to quench your thirst.

THE BEER: Long Trail Brewing Company
5520 US Route 4, Bridgewater Corners
802-672-5011
longtrail.com

Long Trail was the first long-distance trail in the United States. Blazed by the Green Mountain Club between 1910 and 1930, the Long Trail runs 272 miles, slicing across the state of Vermont from Massachusetts to the Canadian border, passing over and through some of the most beautiful mountains on Earth. It was the inspiration for the Appalachian Trail, and over the years it has inspired generations of hikers, wanderers, and explorers and, yes, a brewery.

Joe Buswell & Harry Gorman, Vermont Spirirts

In 1989, the craft-brewing industry in America was still young, and Vermont had not yet become a major player on the scene. That was the year Andy Pherson founded what would become the **Long Trail Brewing Company** in the basement of the Bridgewater Woolen Mill. Pherson wanted to brew an affordable alternative to the pricey German and English beers that American beer lovers were drawn to at the time. He called his small brewery Mountain Brewers and released Long Trail Ale, a full-bodied amber ale modeled after the altbiers of Germany. The beer became popular at local bars and restaurants, and that popularity continued to grow as beer drinkers fell in love with Long Trail's unique offerings.

The brewery moved to its current facility in the mid-1990s and changed its name to reflect its most popular product. The impressive brewery and visiting center were inspired by the Hofbräuhaus in Munich, Germany, a legendary royal Bavarian beer hall. On the banks of the Ottauquechee River, the brewery offers visitors a cool pint of laid-back Vermont country living. In the warmer months guests can enjoy the large deck and beer garden overlooking the river, and it's not uncommon, or frowned upon, for some to wade into the shallow waters holding a glass of beer. In the winter, it is packed with skiers and other cold-sport adventurers who flock to the region.

The large taproom has a big wooden bar area. In addition to a great selection of Long Trail beers on tap, there is also a full offering of pub favorites with locally sourced items and a menu that changes seasonally, based on what is fresh. Though standard brewery tours aren't offered, there is an observation deck that cuts over the brewery where guests can take a self-guided tour.

As soon as you get a glimpse of the brewing space, you understand why tours aren't offered. There just isn't enough room. The brewery is the most overcrowded I've seen in New England; giant fermentation tanks sit in close proximity to one another, while a bottling line whirls with constant motion. Even as big and busy as the brewery is, it can't keep up with the demand for Long Trail products, so a large portion of the brand's beer is brewed at **Otter Creek Brewing Company** (793 Exchange St., Middlebury; 802-388-0727; ottercreekbrewing.com), which is owned by Long Trail and also is a fun brewery to visit during your Vermont travels.

At the Long Trail brewery, guests can enjoy year-round and seasonal Long Trail favorites, as well as access to a brewery-only release called the Farmhouse Series. These beers are named because they're brewed in a pilot system at a small farmhouse on the grounds of the brewery's complex. Experimental and creative, the popular beers in this series occasionally are released outside the brewery as part of a special release or the brewery's Brown Bag draught-only series.

A visit to Long Trail is everything you'd expect: The brewery is big and impressive in terms of its scale and size, and allows fans a chance to experience the source of the products they love. It's a trail worth treading.

On Tap

Longtime favorite

The beer that put Long Trail on the map in 1989 was the **Long Trail Ale.** A quarter of a century later, the full-bodied amber ale with a clean, crisp flavor remains a regional favorite. Those who taste it know exactly why.

ABV: 5% IBUs: 28

Old bag

The older, darker brother to Long Trail Ale is known as **Double Bag.** This beer started the brewery's Brown Bag Series (so named because in its early days, the company didn't have money for new tap handles, so experimental brews would be put on tap at the brewery with a brown bag over the tap handle). This double altbier features a distinct malt presence balanced by a subtle hop backbone for a smooth. complex drink.

ABV: 7.2% IBUs: 39

Do the limbo

The **Limbo IPA** is the first year-round beer Long Trail offers that was born out of the Farmhouse Series after the brewery-only IPAs released in the series proved to be extremely popular. This powerful—and we mean powerful—IPA has 80 IBUs and an intense hop flavor that will have hopheads grinning from ear to ear.

ABV: 7.6% IBUs: 80

THE BOOZE: Vermont Spirits
5573 Woodstock Road (US Route 4), Quechee
802-281-6389
vermontspirits.com

On the side of Route 4 in Quechee, nestled along rolling mountain roads mere yards from the Quechee Gorge, sits the **Vermont Spirits** distillery and sampling room. The distillery is located within the **Quechee Gorge Village,** an old-fashioned country mall that hearkens back to a simpler place and time. From the outside, Vermont Spirits fits that motif perfectly; it's a rustic, barn-like building adorned with the maple tree logo of Vermont Spirits and the American and Canadian flags. Inside, however, the distillery is all about modern innovation, both in terms of the type of spirits it produces and the equipment used to produce them.

The distillery makes one of the world's only vodkas distilled from whey, the natural sugar source found in cow's milk (many other distilleries have tried unsuccessfully to do so). There's a vodka made from the sap of maple trees and one distilled from Vermont apples. The distillery also makes a bourbon, several brandies, a whiskey, and a gin, but it's the vodka that president Steve Johnson tells people to try first during distillery visits.

"I recommend sampling at least two of our three vodkas," he says. "These three really go a long way [toward] explaining the importance of, and reason for, using locally grown agriculture for our primary sugar sources. All three vodkas are exceptional, and they also help to break the thinking that vodka can only be distilled from grain or potatoes."

The distillery is on the smaller side and has far less of a warehouse feel than many other distilleries or breweries. Guests enter through a tasting and gift shop area where they can purchase bottles and try samples, but choose your samples carefully—Vermont Spirits' liquor license only allows samples as large as one-quarter ounce, with each person limited to a total of one ounce of alcohol. In plain English, that means you can only sample four spirits per visit . . . and that's quite sobering.

Although no tours are offered, a large open doorway lets guests see into the distilling area, and staff members are happy to answer questions about the process. Through this open doorway you can see the distillery's unusual equipment, which is part of what Johnson believes is the secret to the place's success.

"What sets us apart from other micro-distillers is how we build and use our columns," he says. "Most of the equipment you see is designed by us and also built by us; this custom fabrication really lets us develop techniques the way we need them and not have to rely on standard design and methods. For example, our one-of-a-kind glass fractionating column allows us to operate as one would in a laboratory, and therefore control outcomes on a much greater level than with a traditional stainless or copper column."

Because there are no tours and a cap on sampling, a trip to this distillery is generally on the shorter side, twenty to thirty minutes, tops. But it's a worthwhile trip, and one that will let you taste some innovative products that remain on the cutting edge of Vermont's craft-distilling world.

Signature Booze

Very sappy

Vermont Gold is a delicate vodka distilled from the sap of maple trees, Vermont's signature flavor. It is batch-distilled in a glass fractionating column and lightly filtered to allow the maple fermentation to shine through in the final product. The result is a vodka with distinctive maple sweetness as well as clear alcohol notes.

Strength: 80 proof

Out of my whey

Vermont White is one of the few spirits distilled from whey. Select nutrients and yeasts are introduced during its distillation to create the lactose fermentation. After distillation in the glass fractioning column still, Vermont springwater and a light charcoal filtration complete the process. The unusual method results in a distinctive vodka with smoothness from start to finish.

Strength: 80 proof

More maple

No. 14 Bourbon unites two American classics—bourbon whiskey and Vermont maple syrup. The strength of this five-year-old bourbon is softened by the sweetness of the maple syrup, making it more accessible.

Strength: 90 proof

Beyond the Beverages

Where to Eat
Long Trail has a full menu with bar-food favorites like fries, wings, and burgers. However, if you're in the mood for something else, another solid option in the area is the **Simon Pearce Restaurant** (1760 Main St., Quechee; 802-295-1470; simonpearce. com). This farm-to-table restaurant has spectacular views of a nearby waterfall.

Tapped Out / Where to Stay
If you want to spend more than one day exploring the natural beauty the area has to offer, local lodging includes the **Quality Inn** at Quechee Gorge (5817 Woodstock Road, US Route 4, Quechee; 802-295-7600; qualityinn.com) and the **October Country Inn** (362 Upper Road, Bridgewater Corners; 802-672-3412; octobercountryinn.com).

Solid Side Trips
Vermont Spirits is part of **Quechee Gorge Village** (5573 Woodstock Road, US Route 4, Quechee; 802-295-1550; quecheegorge.com). Home to **Cabot Quechee Store, Danforth Pewter,** the **Vermont Toy & Train Museum,** and more, this rustic grouping of stores and antiques malls is quintessential Vermont.

The **Vermont Institute of Natural Science** (6565 Woodstock Road, US Route 4, Quechee; 802-359-5000; vinsweb.org) is for the birds—literally. Located on a 47-acre campus adjacent to Quechee State Park, the institute, which is dedicated to environmental education and avian rehabilitation, is open year-round and allows guests an up-close view of the more than forty eagles, falcons, and owls that live there.

Fresh Air

Local cab companies include the White River Junction–based **Big Yellow Taxi** (802-281-8294). There are plenty of walking options in the area, so bring your hiking boots.

Across the street from Vermont Spirits is the **Quechee Gorge at the Quechee State Park** (5800 Woodstock Road, Hartford; 802-295-2990; vtstateparks.com). The gorge is referred to as "Vermont's Grand Canyon" by locals, and while that might be an overstatement, it is grand. The deepest gorge in Vermont, it was formed by glacier activity thirteen thousand years ago. Trails run alongside, offering excellent views of the **Ottauquechee River** flowing 165 feet below, making it clear why this site draws hundreds of thousands of visitors each year. The park has a campground, which is also a great overnight option. This chapter would not be complete without mentioning the **Long Trail**, a 272-mile hiking trail that runs the length of Vermont, and for which Long Trail Brewing Company is named. The trail can be accessed at a variety of points; for details call 802-244-7037, or visit greenmountainclub.org.

Saxtons River Distillery

Hermit Thrush Brewery

Brattleboro

The Trip

An hour from Springfield, Massachusetts, an hour and a half from Hartford, Connecticut, and about two hours from Boston, this charming and eccentric southeastern Vermont town offers a lot of great beverage attractions and is an excellent day trip for those who want to enjoy the spirit of Vermont without venturing too far north. During my trip, I visited **Hermit Thrush Brewery**, walked across the street to **Mocha Joe's Café**, and headed a few minutes outside of downtown to stop in at **Saxtons River Distillery**. I also enjoyed some downtown side trips to Brattleboro brew pubs **Whetstone Station** and **McNeill's Brewery**. Pair them with some great hikes to enjoy the natural beauty of Vermont, and you have a recipe for an excellent day.

THE BEER: Hermit Thrush Brewery
29 High St., Suite 101C, Brattleboro
802-257-2337
hermitthrushbrewery.com

Sour is the new hops—or, at least, it might be.

"Sour beers are possibly the next IPA," says Christophe Gagné, the young, enthusiastic brewer and president behind **Hermit Thrush Brewery**, a new Vermont brewery he opened in late 2014 with Avery Schwenk, his friend and the company's vice president. The brewery is dedicated to Belgian-style beers, including the increasingly popular sour beers that are created with wild-yeast strains. One of the brewery's flagship beers is Brattlebeer, a sour beer brewed with

The Beer
Hermit Thrush Brewery
Order an on-trend sour (a.k.a. the next IPA).

The Booze
Saxtons River Distillery
Vermont maple-syrup-powered line of spirits.

The Brew
Mocha Joe's Café
Great coffee with a socially conscious international presence.

Saxtons River Distillery

cider and described by Gagné as something of a gateway sour beer, because "it's an accessible sour; it's only slightly tart."

In addition to Brattlebeer, the brewery also offers more aggressively sour beers, including a limited-release Flemish Sour Brown that is, as its description warns, "not for the faint of tongue." When I caught up with Gagné in early 2015, he also was planning to brew a sour IPA.

Beyond sours, Gagné produces a wide range of styles at his brewery. All of the beers use yeast strains that he developed as a home brewer, and invoke the yeast-forward flavors of the Belgian tradition. As you may have guessed from his interest in a sour IPA, some of Gagné's beers have strong hop flavors. They include the High Street Vermont IPA, a beer that seeks to, and does, combine some of the best flavors of Belgian and American brewing. It's hoppy, but not particularly bitter, with most of the beer's hop profile present in the aroma, making this an excellent crossover beer.

This brewery is located in the heart of downtown Brattleboro. Most breweries are found off the beaten path where rent is cheaper, and while that's understandable, it's nice to visit a brewery where you can walk out the door after sampling some brews and stroll to dinner or enjoy some other downtown attractions. In addition to its convenient location, Hermit Thrush is a beautiful brewery with a warm, rustic taproom designed to look like a barn. There is a sliding-glass, barn door that separates the taproom from the brewery, and some of the lights are old kerosene lanterns with electric bulbs installed in them. There's also a large number of barrels for future barrel-aging projects. This warm feel, as well as the quality of the beers offered, makes Hermit Thrush a delightful place to visit.

Beyond its beer and beautiful location, Hermit Thrush Brewery also is dedicated to brewing in an environmentally friendly, green manner. Wood-pellet-powered fires, for example, are used to create the steam that heats the brew kettles.

Gagné and Schwenk are happy to be part of the impressive craft-beverage and artistic scene in Brattleboro. "It's really vibrant," Gagné says. "Brattleboro has a lot of arts going on, in addition to food and music and good beverages. I think that all comes together in its character." Ever since Hermit Thrush came to town, that character has gotten just a little more sour.

On Tap

Sour power

Inspired by the town of Brattleboro, **Brattlebeer** is a distinctive sour ale that is brewed with cider. Fermented spontaneously with a blend of local apple cider, malt, and hops, this is a delicate pale ale that is slightly tart, light-bodied, and dry, with both fruity and malty undertones.

It has a bubbly champagne-like head and is a nice introduction for those who have never tried sour beer, as well as a great tasting brew for those already converted.

ABV: 4% IBUs: 8

On High Street

The **High Street Vermont IPA** is a unique beer that combines Belgian and American traditions into one unusual, but delicious pint. The beer has a hop aroma of herbs, citrus, and passion fruit, followed by a resinous tartness. There also are distinctive barrel characters of wood and wine that balance the golden-amber malt without any of the intense bitterness often found in American IPAs.

ABV: 6.8% IBUs: 35

Brown out

The third flagship beer offered by the brewery is a Belgian-style nut brown called **Brooks Brown.** It is a malty, yet light session ale with a deep nutty and roasted malt flavor and a toasted sesame aroma.

ABV: 8% IBUs: 16

The Call of the Wild Beer

Most sour beers are wild beers and are made by a seemingly mystical process known as spontaneous fermentation. Instead of the carefully controlled yeast strains most mainstream modern beers use, wild beers are fermented with wild yeast and bacteria that is allowed to "infect" the beer through the beer being left open to the elements. Many sour and non-sour wild beers are fermented with the wild yeast strain Brettanomyces, known affectionately to beer lovers as "Brett." Though not particularly sour on its own, Brett produces beers with funky esters, and at a beer bar it's not uncommon to hear a phrase like, "I can't really taste Brett in this beer," or "Brett's presence is overpowering."

Bar Trivia

THE BOOZE: Saxtons River Distillery
485 West River Road, Brattleboro
802-246-1128
saplingliqueur.com

There's a throwback feel as soon as you walk through the doors at this distillery. Standing behind the counter at **Saxtons River Distillery** is owner, chief distiller, and taproom manager Christian Stromberg. With a friendly smile and round glasses, he looks like he could be a village blacksmith. Bluegrass music is playing over the loudspeakers, filling the space with an old-time Americana atmosphere.

As Stromberg leads you through a tasting of his delicious Vermont maple-syrup-powered line of spirits, he's more than happy to discuss his distilling philosophy and how he's trying to combine Vermont and American distilling traditions with his Lithuanian heritage.

His family fled czarist-controlled Lithuania in 1906. Although they wished to assimilate into American society, they kept alive many customs from their native country, including that of making flavorful liqueurs. Growing up, Stromberg was familiar with the family tradition but didn't dabble in it professionally, at least not at first. An engineer by trade, he spent more than a dozen years working for Pratt & Whitney in Connecticut before settling in the Brattleboro area. Once in Vermont, Stromberg began to visit the maple sugar houses of friends and gained an appreciation for the hard work that goes into harvesting maple sap and turning it into syrup.

He came up with the idea of making a liqueur in the tradition of the Krupnikas, a Lithuanian and Eastern European liqueur, but sweetened it with maple syrup instead of the traditional honey. The process began as a hobby. "I was playing with it and making fun little batches that I gave away as gifts and things," he recalls. Soon, he had a potential business.

Stromberg opened his business in the barn of his Cambridgeport home on the Saxtons River in 2006. This was before the new wave of craft distilleries started sweeping through New England and much of the nation. It quickly became clear that Stromberg was ahead of his time, and that his maple-powered spirits were a hit with drinkers. Before long, he moved to his current location. The distillery offers a line of Sapling Maple products including a liqueur, bourbon, and rye, as well as a separate coffee liqueur. Besides Vermont, as of 2015 they were available in California, Connecticut, Maine, Massachusetts, Nevada, New Hampshire, and New Jersey.

Unlike many maple-flavored drinks, Stromberg's products use actual maple syrup, not sugar that is flavored like maple syrup. However, he doesn't use maple syrup to ferment his alcohol. Some distilleries do so, but it's expensive, and he claims it doesn't add to the flavor and is not in keeping with the make-do and do-without spirit of distilling history. Either way, it's a history that seems alive and well in his hands.

Signature Booze

Sappy

Featuring select, locally harvested, Vermont Grade A maple syrup, *Sapling Maple Liqueur* is bold, smooth, and never too sweet despite its maple flavor.
Strength: 70 proof

Sweet, sweet bourbon

The Sapling Maple Bourbon is a maple-infused spirit that starts with three-year-old bourbon that is then blended with maple syrup and aged a second time in American oak barrels. The result is a rich bourbon with a light maple finish.
Strength: 70 proof

Perk up

Perc Coffee Liqueur uses organic Arabica coffee beans imported from Central America and roasted in small batches. The coffee flavor is balanced with natural cane sugar, yielding a rich flavor that, like Saxtons River's other products, is sweet but not overly so.
Strength: 60 proof

THE BREW: Mocha Joe's Café
82 Main St., Brattleboro
802-257-7794
mochajoes.com

Mocha Joe's Café is located on a sloping street, sitting halfway underground. For more than two decades, this classic coffeehouse has served high-quality cups of joe to the huddled masses of Brattleboro. What started as a humble coffeehouse in 1991 has become a local institution—and a roasting powerhouse with a socially conscious international presence. These lofty goals were not part of the cafe's original business model, says owner Ellen Capy. When she and husband Pierre opened their doors, all they wanted to do was offer great coffee.

"We both worked for the Coffee Connection in Boston," Ellen recalls. Coffee Connection was a revolutionary Boston company that helped bring high-end coffee to the East Coast, originated the Frappuccino (Starbucks later purchased it), and popularized the notion of single-origin coffee. The Capys' love of fine coffee was fostered there as they learned the art and science behind the beverage.

In the early 1990s, Pierre's mother convinced him to return to his native Brattleboro, and it was in this historic Vermont city that the couple made their mark on the craft-beverage world of New England. When they opened, Ellen says, the average consumer was less sophisticated about coffee. "People didn't even know what a latte was," she recalls.

Although customers may not have known the name of what they were drinking, they knew it tasted good, and Mocha Joe's thrived. For its first few years the shop purchased its coffee from the Coffee Connection, but in 1994 Starbucks purchased Coffee Connection and Mocha Joe's launched its own small roastery. The roastery initially was created to provide fresh roasted beans for the coffeehouse, but requests from other businesses began to come in, so before long the roastery was distributing locally, then nationally, and then internationally.

A couple of blocks away from Mocha Joe's coffeehouse is the company's beautiful roastery. It's not open to the public, but informal classes are offered there for clients of the roastery and baristas in training. Coffee lovers can go online to order various coffees and blends with beans from different countries.

In the years since the company opened, Pierre has traveled to coffee-producing regions many times and has helped to foster direct relationships between roasters and farmers in the country of origin. The roastery also is working with farmers in Cameroon with the goal, Ellen says, for Mocha Joe's to become the first US importer of high-end coffee from the country.

Get a taste of their newest discovery next time you're cruising through Brattleboro.

Signature Brews

Café coffee

It's hard to go wrong with any of the drink options offered at Mocha Joe's Café, but my favorites are the *cappuccino*—made with two types of Brazilian beans blended together —and the standard house-blend *drip coffees*, which rotate seasonally, but always include a dark roast and a regular roast.

Sugar magnolia

The roastery's *Costa Rican La Magnolia* uses beans from the renowned Costa Rican La Minita estate. Smooth and rich, this medium roast has a nice balance of sweetness and body.

Espresso yourself

The Italian-style *Espresso Blend* was developed after years of experimentation. It has intense high notes and a lingering dark-chocolate base. It's perfect for shots or mixed drinks.

Beyond the Beverages

Where to Eat

Beer lovers will want to make a beeline for **Whetstone Station** (36 Bridge St., Brattleboro; 802-490-2354; whetstonestation.com). Located downtown on the banks of the Connecticut River, this restaurant and brewery is a craft-beverage destination in its own right. It is home to a 3.5-barrel nanobrewery that specializes in producing a constantly changing array of experimental beers that are interesting and flavorful. (All of the beer recipes produced at the restaurant are open-source and posted on the website for home brewers to duplicate.) In addition to the house-made beers, there's also an extensive beer list featuring Vermont beers, as well as national and international offerings. On top of all that, the food is excellent, with a menu that changes seasonally and is based on local ingredients.

Another nearby dining option is the intimate and eccentric **T. J. Buckley's** (132 Elliot St., Brattleboro; 802-257-4922) that is housed in a vintage dining car. This restaurant does not take credit or debit cards, so don't spend all your cash at the brewery or bar. It also only seats about eighteen people, so reservations are a must.

Tapped Out / Where to Stay

There are several hotel options in the area, but if you want the true Brattleboro experience, with all the quirks and charm the town has to offer, look no further than the **Latchis Hotel and Theatre** (50 Main St., Brattleboro; 802-254-6300; latchis.com). Part of the Latchis Memorial Building, built in 1938 as "A Town within a Town—Under One Roof," this hotel is an Art Deco treasure. Some of the rooms have water views, and you're close to Brattleboro's downtown action. In the same building as the hotel is the Latchis Theatre, a movie venue and performing arts center with four theaters, one of which is a grand old movie palace, complete with Greek statues and hand-painted murals depicting scenes from Greek mythology.

Solid Side Trips

Beyond the three liquid destinations featured in this chapter, beer lovers will want to make time to check out the town's two brew pubs, the aforementioned Whetstone Station and **McNeill's Brewery** (90 Elliot St., Brattleboro; 802-254-2553). Opened in 1989–90, this pioneering brew pub is one of the most beloved in all of New England, and has a legendary status with older lovers of craft beer. When I was a kid it was one of my dad's favorite haunts, so our frequent family day trips to Brattleboro would inevitably conclude at this classic-style pub with long tables.

Over the years the word on the street (a.k.a., beer websites) was that founder and original brewer Ray McNeill had taken a step away from the business, but by the time I visited in early 2015, he was back firmly at the helm. A variety of English- and German-style beers were available, as well as several cask-conditioned beers. The beers I tasted, including the **Extra Special Bitter**, were complex and excellent. Due to the rise of great breweries across New England since the 1990s, McNeill's offerings are, through no fault of their own, less earth-shattering than they once were. It still remains a classic brew pub worth visiting. The beer here provides a taste of brewing history, and a pretty darn tasty one at that.

Fresh Air

Other than Saxtons River Distillery, the Brattleboro craft-beverage attractions featured in this chapter are all conveniently located downtown, within walking distance of one another. So you can "walk off" the aftereffects of your craft-beer adventures while window-shopping and exploring the town. If you need a ride to or from the distillery or are staying at a hotel outside of downtown, call **Brattleboro Taxi** (802-254-6446; brattleborotaxi. com). If a more-intense hike is what you have in mind, check out the **Retreat Trails,** a two-trail system totaling more than eleven miles. You can access these trails from Route 30 north of downtown at the Retreat Farm and Grafton Village Cheese.

Blazed decades ago on the grounds of Vermont's first facility to treat psychiatric patients, which opened in 1834, the trails have mostly moderate grades that are great for hiking and mountain-biking. One trail will take you past the **Retreat Tower,** a fairy-tale-style edifice of stone that was built by patients. The tower is closed to the public; according to unverified local lore, it's because over the years it became a popular suicide destination for patients at the hospital. Cue the horror-movie pipe-organ soundtrack.

Another Round: Vermont

Hill Farmstead Brewery
403 Hill Road, Greensboro Bend
802-533-7450
hillfarmstead.com

Kiss the ground, because a visit here is a trip to the Jerusalem of New England brewing. This brewery was rated as the best in the world on Ratebeer.com on multiple occasions, and the wait to get in is generally one to four hours. Is it really worth it? If you love beer, it probably is.

The beer from Hill Farmstead is available, for the most part, only at the brewery and a select number of Vermont bars. Kegs also occasionally make their way into places like New York and Philadelphia. While you're in Vermont, you can usually find Hill Farmstead beers available at the **Farmhouse Tap and Grill** in Burlington (see Burlington chapter). Bottom line: Whether you visit to the brewery or not, if you see this beer at a bar in Vermont or someplace else, order it.

Lawson's Finest Liquids
802-272-8436
lawsonsfinest.com

This is another brewery that you can't visit (it's small, and in a residential neighborhood), but nevertheless it's the source of some incredible and hard-to-find beer. (That will change soon, as Lawson's announced plans to open a bigger brewery and tasting room in Waitsfield, Vermont.) Look for brews such as the aptly named **Sip of Sunshine IPA**, as refreshing as a summer's day, and the **Fayston Maple Imperial Stout**, brewed with about two gallons of Vermont maple syrup and then aged for over a year in rum barrels. In 2014, Lawson's Finest began doing some contract-brewing at **Two Roads Brewing Company** in Stratford, Connecticut (see Bridgeport and Stratford chapter), which made the brewery's beer somewhat more available outside of Vermont, but it's still difficult to find.

Switchback Brewing Company
160 Flynn Ave., Burlington
802-651-4114, switchbackvt.com

This is yet another excellent brewery in Burlington. It has a sleek taproom that is generally hopping (just had to use that pun one more time) on the weekends, and often features live music. The beer itself is approachable and never disappoints. This is a worthy stop on the Burlington leg of your craft beverage journeys.

The Alchemist
Waterbury
alchemistbeer.com

There is no address listed because this brewery is not open to the public. I'm writing about it because no book that claimed to cover Vermont craft beverages would be complete without mention of the holy grail of beer produced by this brewery, **Heady Topper**. This flavorful double IPA is often hailed as the best beer in the world (The Alchemist and Hill Farmstead are locked in a close race for world brewing supremacy). Topper is nearly impossible to find outside of Vermont, and pretty darn difficult to find even in Vermont. Reportedly it's been sold on the black market in Washington, D.C., for as much as $18 a can. If you're traveling in Vermont, keep your eyes open for this beer, and if you happen to see any, buy some for me.

The Farmhouse Tap and Grill
Photo by Brian Eckert

Glossary

Don't worry, there won't be a quiz, but here is a collection of some beer, coffee, and spirit terms you may have encountered in this book.

Beer Terms

Alcohol by volume (ABV): The amount of alcohol in a beverage; a higher ABV indicates a higher alcohol content.

Esters: Flavor compounds that form during fermentation and contribute to the fruity aroma and flavor of beer.

Flights: A set, usually four or more, of beer samples.

Growler(s): A glass jug used to take draught beer home from a brewery. You can purchase a growler or half-growler at most breweries, or bring your own.

Hops: The cone-shaped female flowers of the hop plant and a common flavoring agent in beer that gives it its bitterness, and other flavors. Hop varieties have different flavors, and some beers are brewed with a variety of hops.

International Bitterness Units (IBUs): The measure of the bittering substances in beer. The higher the IBU, the more bitter-tasting the brew. Budweiser has an extremely low IBU rating of 8; in contrast, the popular (and not particularly bitter) craft beer, Sierra Nevada Pale Ale, has an IBU of 35. Some beers can have IBUs as high as 80, or more.

Saison: A loosely defined style of farmhouse ale that originated in France. Many are very fruity in the aroma and flavor, with lots of spice and a medium bitterness.

Session beer: A beer with a low ABV that you can drink over a period of time, or a "session," without getting drunk.

Sessionable: A good session beer.

Booze Terms

Distillation: A process by which a fermented drink, including beer or wine, is purified and diluting elements like water are eliminated.

Neat: A drink served straight from the bottle without ice or any additional ingredients.

Pot still: A type of still where heat is applied directly to the pot containing the wash.

Proof: A measure of how much alcohol is contained in an alcoholic beverage. Generally used when discussing spirits instead of ABV. In the United States, a beverage's proof is roughly twice its percentage of ABV (i.e., a beer that has 10 percent ABV is about 20 proof).

The wash: The fermented liquid that exists prior to distillation. In whiskey the wash is usually a type of un-hopped beer.

Brew Terms

Coffee blends: A coffee that is made from a variety of beans. Often each bean is chosen because of a specific characteristic, and the blend combines these various characteristics to create a desired flavor and consistency.

Espresso: Strong coffee made by forcing steam through ground coffee beans. It is used in espresso bar drinks like a cappuccino or a latte. Espresso is often made from dark-roast coffee, but it can also be made from a light roast.

Manual brew: Coffee that is essentially made by hand under the complete control of the coffee maker. Includes pour-overs and French-press coffee.

Pour-over: A type of coffee brewing where a barista (or anyone making coffee with this method) pours hot water into the filter by hand, thereby controlling the coffee-making process, usually delivering a measured amount of liquid over a period of a few minutes which can bring out distinctive, bright, and sweet flavors in the coffee.

Terroir: The environmental conditions, particularly soil and climate, that give an agricultural product such as coffee beans, wine grapes, hops, or apples their flavor.

Last Call

We've made it.

There some wrong turns, unintended detours, one or two spills and perhaps, upon occasion, a sample or two too many, but if you're reading this, like me, you've been through the promised land of the New England beverage world and lived to tell the tale. And what a tale it has been.

If you visited all or some of my suggested destinations, odds are you've consumed some of the best coffee, beer, and spirits found anywhere in the world, and you've come away with epic stories, full growlers, and perhaps a new friend or two.

Along the way I'm sure you've also formed your own opinion about the proper technique for a pourover coffee, the right level of botanicals a truly great gin should contain, and just where you fall on the sour beer divide (most of us either hate or love this style). And if you're like me, the craft beverage journey is far from over because the quest for craft beverage nirvana is ongoing. In addition to printed and online advise, I also encourage craft beverage explorers to never overlook good ole' fashioned word of mouth. I've found craft lovers are a vocal group and more than happy to share their favorite places. To that end, if there's any New England watering holes, favorite beverages, or little known hot spots you feel I've overlooked let me know either through Islandport Press or on Social Media (my name is fairly distinctive, so I'm easy to find on Twitter and other sites). Believe me when I say I will do my damndest to checkout these recommendations as soon as is humanly possible.

Until then, I hope you've enjoyed your craft beverage exploration and wish you all the best in future adventures. As they say at some point after midnight at bars across the country, "you don't have to go home but you can't stay here."

Tasting Notes